THE SELF-ESTEEM FORMULA

HOW TO OVERCOME LOW SELF-ESTEEM AND CREATE A HIGHER ONE!

BHUPINDER SANDHU

"You alone are enough.
You have nothing to prove to anyone."

Maya Angelo

Work like you don't need the money.
Love like you've never been hurt.
Dance like nobody's watching.

For the amazing gifts of life and love,
I dedicate this book to my loving mother,
Ninderjit Kaur

No part of this book may be reproduced in any form.

The information presented herein represents the view of the author as of date of publication. This book is presented information only.

Index

Acknowledgements

We all need a cheering squad to root upon, and I'm blessed to have great cheerleaders in my life. They are: Chandan, my partner in crime, my dynamic loving life partner, she is my biggest critic and supporter, she never complained for the times I spent in my study while writing this book, without her support this project would have never seen the light; Jamal Anderson, the fist editor of this book, without his valuable suggestions, I would have missed many interesting insights; Amrit, my sweet sister-in-law, who has always been encouraging and available to me, her appreciation of my work fills my heart. Ahmad Junaid, first person to encourage me to walk on the journey of self-development. Rupinder Parmar and Bhupinder Sohi, my best friends who have always supported me in everything I did, no questions asked.

Last but not the least my dad Sh. Meetpal Sandhu, from whom I learnt the never give up attitude.

8

Introduction

Introduction

When you are born, with a specific gender, you all are given a name, a nationality, a race, and an identity. But you understand none of these labels as an infant or as a child, and none of these come even remotely close to capturing your true essence. With every passing day, you start categorizing these labels more intricately.

Every person you've come across, portrayed his or her ideas or opinions of what those labels should mean. And because there were so many opinions voiced with so much conviction, you eventually started believing in them and soon they became your reality. Since you grew up with such strong persuasions that today you stand up with them, as your real self. You are trying to live up to that image of yourself, which was created by you; without real you in it. This picture of yours is painted with the labels and opinions (paint and brush) of others. The more you identify with the idea of your real-self, the more you would inevitably feel insecure and worthless, because no man or woman could live up to an image which is eclipsed by others' perception.

Dear reader - you are NOT an image or a concept of even an entity. You need to paint picture of real you with your own paint and brush, on a clean canvas as you were at the time of your birth.

The part of you that you are identifying with, is constantly in a state of flux. Your thoughts don't stay the same. Your perspectives keep changing. Your feelings are continually fading and flowing, moving from one state to another and so on – till you fall asleep and finally the day you die. Ironically, these changes are also not independent, they are also by-product of some external input.

So, to identify yourself with what is constantly coming and going is to identify yourself with what isn't real you. After all, you don't go when your feelings go, do you? You don't change when your mood changes, do you? What you have here is a case of a misunderstood identity. You have identified yourself with the wrong picture.

You are not what you consider yourself to be. You are not, you have phenomenal potential to create what you want, and you had it the day you were born. It just got covered by the layers of labels from the society, but you have the power to crack those layers and shine the unstoppable you, the real you.

But as long as you believe in the picture painted by others, you can never convince yourself that you are worthy of higher and better things. The belief that you are not entitled to higher things has to be changed. You have to dis-identify yourself from this and associate with the better version.

So, who are you then? / Now, how will you describe yourself?

Certainly, you are at the Shakespearean's first stage of infancy, mewling and puking in nurse's arms, oblivious to your true-self. You could not find your true self in the world of thoughts and you cannot form your authentic image on mere thoughts and concepts of others because these concepts pre-existed before you were born.

If you could not be found in thoughts, where could you be found? Who are you when you forget to think about yourself? Who are you when you are immersed in a stimulating conversation, a good book, or a fun activity?

You could not be reduced to words and concepts. You are perfect and has always strived to be perfect. You are your best self. You are simply who you are and have always been. The belief that you have no self-esteem or self-worth is not a reality, because self-esteem and self-worth are simply concepts and labels.

Now let's talk briefly about what self-esteem is, before we move further and discuss the pieces of equation that would help you to attach improved labels to the label of "Self-Esteem".

In simple words self-esteem refers to the amount of realistic respect you have for yourself. To lead a happy and successful life, both emotionally and physically, one needs to have a healthy self-esteem. People with low self-esteem often have more difficulty leading a life of affluence. People with nourishing self-esteem appreciate to be credited with everything good in their lives, while those who suffer from low self-esteem feel that they don't deserve the same. Hence each person is responsible for his own self-esteem and could even take steps to recuperate it further, as a result improving his life and the lives of the people around him.

Your self-esteem is not static, it develops throughout life. It seems to be a great news as you can change it with jiff of guidance and your will power. Your childhood experiences play a major role in determining whether as an adult, you have healthy self-esteem or low self-esteem. People who have healthy self-esteem have often been applauded in their childhood undertakings for displaying high spirits, exhibiting their best demeanour amidst their parents and others who play an important role in their lives, being cynosures and great source of attraction of their loved ones with triumphant glories in school and sports and have a big list of trusted friends.

Children who grow up with low self-esteem often have experience precisely contrary to the ones mentioned above. They are prone to harsh criticism, no matter how hard they try, they are often shouted and even smacked at times, ignored, ridiculed or mocked at, by those in authority. As in pairs, their high expectant parents other than boosting up their morals, dampen their spirits thus labelling them to be lifetime failures. Low self-esteem could affect both one's mental and physical health. If you suffer from low self-esteem, you should explore options that help you improve your self-esteem, which in turn would improve your quality of life.

Happiness and Optimism

Chapter 1

Happiness and Optimism

What is your life perspective? It is how you see or perceive the world around you, how you see or perceive life and more specifically your own life. How you perceive your life, that is, your life perspective would directly affect how you think, feel and act. How you think, feel and act would naturally determine how your life ends. Simply the perspective of life is an important component in the process of creating higher self-esteem.

Changing Perspective, changed Life!

Your perspective and attitude towards life in general plays an important role in how happy you are in life and the success you have. If you think positively about life situation, people and objects, then you would be comparatively more relaxed, calm than someone who is always looking at the dark side of things, coz stress encapsulates them, and they remain under constant pressure.

The way you think and feel not only affects you, but also affects those around you, in short, our mood affects our day and accumulation of these days affects your life. Developing and maintaining a positive perspective is essential if you want to lead a positive and blissful life.

"You see, what you look for!"

There are many ways in which you could develop a more positive perspective and begin to change your way of thinking and feeling about many situations you encounter in everyday life. Changing your attitude and not falling back into negative thoughts would take time, but eventually the new perspective would become second nature. The four main key points to remember to change your perspective are:

- First and foremost, change that you have to bring is to think positively, no matter what the situation is. Prefer monotasking and concentrate on completing one task at a time. Look for positive results and how good you feel when you have completed the task. Never give in to doubts and let yourself believe that you have assumed too much and move on.

- Always look for the positive in those around you which would encourage a positive attitude around you. Regular practice of this would have a ripple effect. Like when you spray perfume on others, you are likely to drop few on yourself.

- Whatever you are doing in your daily life always look for the good in it, no matter how monotonous the task is. The more you despise your work the more negativity it breeds in you. Try to find something about it that results in a more positive situation. Changing your perspective about the thing would change your feeling, which in turn could be a new beginning of liking the same job.

- As we are programmed for negativity, going downhill is always easy. That is why never let yourself be distracted or deceived to return to negativity, it takes time to change the way you feel and think. As you have been impressed upon by the negativity of the world for a long time, your new perspective would take time to register and stay.

Over time you would discover that many areas of your life will change simply by changing your perspective from a negative to a better positive one. You'll discover that your self-esteem recuperates, becomes more acceptable, you feel happier and more confident than before, and are able to tackle the tasks effortlessly that you detested doing earlier, without causing yourself stress and anxiety These are just some of the areas where you could improve and get a more positive perspective and, therefore, lead a more positive life.

What is your self-esteem?

Realizing your self-esteem has nothing to do with checking your bank balance, your work, your status in society, your family, it's just you, and the person you are in life. You give respect, love and consideration to others, but how often do you give yourself what you owe? How you value yourself is based on the self-esteem you have; your self-esteem estimates to what magnitude you value yourself. Building healthy self-esteem in oneself primes to independence, happiness, and flexibility, the ability to easily adapt to change, cooperation and a positive outlook in any situation. On the other hand, low unhealthy self-esteem only leads to irrational thoughts, unhappiness, fear of the new, rigidity, defensive attitude and a negative outlook towards life in general.

The way we see ourselves pictures the perspective of others towards us. For instance, if we are happy, smiling and full of confidence, then others see us as someone they want to be with. If we depict this feature of self-respect for ourselves, we are certainly bound to be respected by others. After all, how could you ask others to respect you if you don't respect yourself? So, finding and mounting your self-esteem is all about developing it. So, let's take a look at the esteem.

High self-esteem

People with high self-esteem clearly indicate who they are, to what direction they are destined to and their stark commitment towards their goal. They accept responsibility and the consequences of their actions instead of blaming others or excusing themselves. They are not self-centred, but care about the welfare of others. They are goal oriented, productive, creative and optimistic. And, most importantly, a person with healthy self-esteem understands that he/she is worthy of being loved and cared for, as well as loving and caring for others.

If you have high self-esteem, you will see certain traits in yourself and how you look, the traits related to high self-esteem are:

- You know who you are and have confidence in your abilities.

- You will always express your true feelings to others.

- Your relationship with others will be smooth and appreciable.

- You'll recognize yourself and take pride in your achievements in life.

- You can easily forgive yourself for mistakes and also forgive others.

Low self-esteem

People with low self-esteem often crave the approval of those around them. They have a poor history at school or work. They are poor problem solvers and barely take chances. They often have irrational beliefs and tend to think unreasonably in critical situations. People with low self-esteem often face the day with many fears, the main one is the fear of rejection from others. They are often insecure, anxious, and nervous and may overreact and exhibit resentment and anger if they feel that someone does not accept them. They don't hold themselves responsible for their wrong actions rather shoulder blame others. Most importantly, a person with low self-esteem does not feel worthy of giving or receiving love, affection and compassion.

Similarly, if you have problems with self-esteem or low self-esteem, then a certain pattern will follow in your thoughts and forms. Unfortunately, you are defined as a person of low self - esteem if you can identify yourself with the facts mentioned below:

- Not believing in yourself makes you self-doubting and insecure.

- You have difficulty in accepting and getting involved in intimate relationships.

• You never allow your real feelings surface; therefore, you live a pretentious life.

• You mostly fail in giving due credit to yourself as you are unable to acknowledge your accomplishments.

• You take things personally and too seriously, because of this you have the inability to forgive others and especially yourself.

• You are so stuck in your ways that you are scared of change and resist change at every opportunity with all your power.

Developing your self-esteem

There are many ways in which you can increase your self-esteem and change to a more positive and healthy perspective about yourself, here are some tips to develop and increase your self-esteem.

• Do not take other people's criticism seriously, instead listen to what they are saying and learn from it. People see world from their perspective, and not from yours. You have altogether different perception to see the world.

• Take out some time for yourself every day, meditate, look inside yourself and post introspecting yourself, you'll realize your strengths and even strive to work upon your fragile areas where you feel, you cannot stand firm. When you sit with yourself, you start knowing yourself better. You need to talk to yourself, develop a relationship with yourself. Once this relation is established you are less affected by the outer world. Basically, you are in relationship with yourself, which is the most important one in your life.

• Celebrate and take pride in even the smallest achievements you attain. You start running after you have mastered walking. Nothing in life is big or small, your perspective and thinking gives it a shape. So, celebrate your small triumphs and glories which not only gratify your soul but take away the drudgery of your life which you give utmost importance to. Waking up in the morning is a challenge for many. But in my case, its vice versa. My celebration starts as soon as I wake up in the morning. Yes, I start my day by celebrating my waking up in the morning, because I consider myself privileged enough to wake up healthily than not waking up at all.

• Do something every day you like, like taking a walk in the park or soaking in a bubble bath. You were born to do things which you enjoyed but lost your music in the business of the world around you. Start doing something that gives you inner self pleasure and content. Tune into the music of life that you lost. Play the tune you once loved but never heard for years because your partner didn't like it. Wear the dress you never wore in a hope of getting fit which you regrettably couldn't.

• Deprivation is not good for your health and also for your soul. Never deprive yourself of something you enjoy, if you know you shouldn't do it, then do it anyway and stop punishing yourself for it. You have no right to deprive this life of yours from experiencing what it enjoys. You are here on a journey, not to stay forever. So, let loose and take a chill pill. Universe is a miraculous creation; it would never say no to you. Deprivation is in your imagination, not in the universe. Connect to the source.

• The way you speak with others determines the quality of your relationship with them, similarly the way you speak with yourself reflects your relationship with yourself. Therefore, always try to speak positively and respectfully to yourself. Use affirmations to override all the negative thoughts and emotions.

Positive self-talk: The greatest Arsenal

One of the biggest influences you could use to your advantage in life is you, yourself. In particular, you can use your thoughts since they have the power to influence your feelings and emotions. By learning to control your internal dialogue and turn it into a positive internal dialogue instead of a negative one, what most people do unconsciously all the time, you could start to have more control over almost every aspect of your life and would be able to make essential changes.

Your ability to succeed in life depends largely on how you deal with life, a positive mental attitude enables you to lead a more balanced life than a person delimited with grim thoughts which further leads to lack of self-confidence and low self-esteem. By adopting a positive attitude, the meaning of life starts changing and you look at life in a different way leading to optimism and success. Your quality of life is based on how you think and feel from one moment to another and changing your way of thinking could dramatically change the way you see life and treat it.

The person who continues to lead his life optimistically with a positive attitude is better able to deal with life and combat with the problems more assertively and is resilient enough to recuperate from the problems or setbacks that the life challenges him with. The optimistic person would see the problem for what it is, nothing more than a temporary setback that could overcome and move forward, by looking at life in this optimistic way, the person is able to take full control over his thoughts and feelings and has the tendency to alter a negative situation to a positive one simply by altering the way he thinks. Nevertheless, thoughts can be positive or negative and you can only have one thought in mind at a time, choosing positive will keep your thoughts, feelings and actions optimistic, which leads to a happier state and can achieve his goals much more easily.

Using positive self-talk in your daily life

You have been using negative self-talk whole your life, it has been scientifically proved that more than 90% of your self-talk is negative. 90% of our subconscious thinking is negative and we are looking for a positive life, a positive world. There is no fault of yours in this, you have been programmed by the parents, schools and society to be negative. Most of the stuff you read, and watch is negative. You watch "WALKING DEAD" and then expect to walk full of life which is authentically not possible. News media is the biggest source of negativity on this planet.

You have to work hard to erase this program of negativity to create space for the positive program. This could be tiring task, just like cleaning a big house full of junk stored over the years. It is possible, you might need help. You are there to help yourself.

"Journey of 1000 miles start with a single step."

Start with taking small steps, incorporate positive self-talk in your life and practice it throughout the day. This would slowly help you establish a new thinking pattern. The negative thinking pattern that you have established unconsciously over the years would be reprogrammed to positive pattern with time.

To begin with, you should develop a schedule and aim to repeat positive affirmations around 50 times throughout the day, this could be achieved by repeating positive statements quietly to yourself or out aloud. Positive self-talk could be used for many different aspects in your life, it could help you to overcome difficult situations, gain more confidence in yourself, help you to quit habits, recover quicker from illness or make changes in your life in general. Popular phrases or sentences that could be used in positive self-talk include:

- I have an interesting challenge facing me – this could be used when a problem occurs in life or there is some difficulty, rather than looking at the situation in a negative way and thinking I have a problem, thinking of it as a challenge is a much more appreciable and positive way of dealing with it.

- I like the person I am – this could be used to bolster self-confidence and gain respect about yourself and the person you are, similar statements could be "I am the best", "I am a good person" or "I have many excellent qualities".

- I know I could do this – this could be used if you are faced with a certain task that you would previously doubt yourself capable of conquering, similarly you could say "I have the ability to conquer this" or "this doesn't pose a problem for me"

- I am full of health, energy and vitality – this could be used to encourage good feelings about your health either after you have been sick or while recovering from an illness.

- I am fulfilled as a person – this could be used to encourage good general positive thoughts about yourself and the world in which you live.

How positive affirmations could change your life?

Having a positive attitude is the key to being happy and leading a successful life, our thoughts play a huge role in how we feel, and positive thinking leads to a confident person happy in life, while negativity leads to low self-esteem and you missing out on so much in life. We so often talk ourselves out of things without even realizing we are doing so, everyday hundreds of negative thoughts drift freely through our mind, we put ourselves down too much and sow the seeds of doubt. There is a small simple tool that you could use throughout the day to help to ward off these negative thoughts and instil a more positive way of thinking, using daily positive affirmations could change your life drastically for the better. They could make you more confident, more aware, surer of yourself and change your life in many more aspects for the better.

What are positive affirmations?

Positive affirmations could be used throughout the day anywhere and at any time you need them, the more you use them the easier positive thoughts would take over negative ones and you would see benefits happening in your life. An affirmation is a simple technique that is used to change negative self-talk that we are rarely even aware of doing, into looking at your life with a more positive attitude. Most of us have for many years bombarded ourselves with negative thoughts so changing your thoughts and the way you think won't happen overnight but if you stick with affirmations they would work once you have retrained your way of thinking. There are many different affirmation techniques for dealing with different situations in life and the most popular and successful are listed below.

The mirror technique

When you study human behaviour, it's quite clear that we humans tend to bond with or be more attracted to those that are most like ourselves. When someone behaves in a manner that we understand and can relate to, we are more receptive to ideas and opinions that the other person might express. In mirroring behaviour, you take advantage of this innate human quality by intently watching the mannerisms, tone, posture and speaking style of yourself.

This technique helps you to appreciate yourself and develop self-awareness and self-esteem, you stand in front of a mirror, preferably a full length one, so that you can see your entire body. Start from your head and work down on your body, say out loud what you like about the areas of your body, for example, you might say "I like the way my hair shines, the little colour differences where the light hits it "or" the shade of my eyes is appealing and the dynamic sheen they possess can do wonders and enable me to fetch multiple friends." Take time and slowly travel your entire body building a more positive image of yourself.

Basically, you are talking to yourself and appreciating your body parts that you have never noticed or have always overlooked them. This is very common in women, it to happen with men but at a very little scale. Plastic surgery has become a fashion, tampering with your natural gifts is considered imprudence. These are the signs of low self-image that people have about themselves. You need to appreciate your uniqueness, because several studies show that people who go under knife to look better are not happy even after. Most would find something else to feel bad about and this cycle is endless until they develop self -love.

The anywhere technique

This is a very simple yet very powerful technique to carry in your arsenal bag because you never know when the storm of negativity engulfs you. You can use this anywhere and whenever you catch yourself thinking a negative thought. So, what you do is that, when you realize that you are enclosed with negative thought, in your head imagine the volume knob of your music player turning to the full volume and when the negative thought diminishes, with your power of imagination see yourself turning the volume down using the same knob. Keep turning it down till it is low enough that you could not hear it.

It's not finished yet, now you have to think of a positive affirmation, a positive thought or a positive story to replace this negative thought. With your imagination turn the music on and make it loud. Because show must go on, and there is no show without music.

The Burn technique

This is one of my favourite techniques and had done wonders for my clients over the years. We all have good and bad experiences in life, but bad experiences tend to stay with us for long, sometimes for lifetime and they are there to hurt us, give us pain every time they come to surface.

This is a very simple practice and very powerful, believe me it is really potent. You need a pen and a paper, and then a quiet place or your favourite place, best if you are alone (don't try this alone with unbearable emotions that could harm you) and write down the life experience that have caused you pain and is still capable of doing it. The experience brings negativity, sadness, discomfort, sorrow or grief. Now without thinking or giving any power to this experience, write it down, you don't need to think, you don't have to be accurate, don't worry about the grammar, just write in the flow. Write every single detail, every single emotion and every feeling attached to it. Keep writing, you can repeat.

Once you have finished writing, don't read what have you written this is really important. You don't read it because you wrote it to eliminate and reading it would hinder the elimination process.

Last step: if you have fireplace at home, crush this piece of paper and throw it and see it burning, if you don't have fireplace tear and crumple the paper and bin it or use shredder to shred.

Many people question the validity of this process when they hear it first, that how writing on a piece of paper could help eliminating bad experiences. My first encounter with this question happened few years back in a mindfulness retreat, where a lady asked me this question after I had explained this technique.

I was surprised by the question and I went silent for a few moments, may be a minute or so as I didn't have any answer. I didn't have the direct answer then and still don't have one today. But after those moments of silence a story surfaced on the field of my memory which my grandmother told me once.

In school holidays when we went to see her in our village, all 12 of us (my siblings and cousins), she used to tell us stories of my uncles and aunties. We all slept in open under the sky in this big courtyard, there must be around 25 to 30 charpayies (Indian cots) at one time. She used to narrate so many stories and her own experiences which were so gripping and intriguing that everybody wanted his cot next to hers. Being the eldest of all I was lucky one always.

One night I asked her why she has kept all the letters that we all wrote to her, she had kept the first letter of mine which I probably wrote to her about 35 years ago. This was the first letter I wrote to her when I was just 3. I struggled and hardly wrote anything; it was more of a drawing sheet rather than a letter.

She smiled and after few moments, she replied, and I could feel the emotion in her voice. She said these are not just words, these are your emotions, feelings and love for me. She said, "I could feel you in these words, when you are not here, they remind me of your presence in my life, your love." After telling that there were tears in her eyes. The best bit about this whole story is that my grandmother could not read or write. My youngest aunt used to read it for her, and my grandmother remembered every word we wrote.

When I shared this story with the people on my retreat they were able to empathize that the content in a letter carries such a weightage and can have such a powerful impact, it's naturally believable that the saga of your painful experience that you've undergone through, if penned down can persuasively help in unshackling you of the burdens you carried and I'm sure you'll be glad to get it off your chest.

Focus:
The Hidden Key

Chapter: 2

Focus: The Hidden Key

"Where focus goes, energy flows."

Your life is sum total of the objects or things, where you have focused your energy throughout your life. All your success and failures are result of your focus, more focused you are, more successful you are. It is just like water, if you water a piece of land, what will grow. Both flowers and weeds, because water doesn't discriminate between weed and flower. Similarly, energy doesn't discriminate between positive and negative, you focus your energy on positive thing, positivity grows likewise negativity grows if you focus on negatives.

Nobody in this earth has a perfect life, you all experience some tough/rough times in life, it is purely just life; it isn't always supposed to be a bed of roses. None of us were born with certificate from life saying, *"I WILL BE EASY FOR YOU."* If anyone was, then please let me know because I haven't met anyone with this certificate of easy life. But the beauty is that your life is just what you make out of it.

More positivity you develop and incorporate in your life easier it gets to walk on this journey called life. Bad times come but they don't have effect on you, you deal them as another event in life. You don't give it the unnecessary power to this unhealthy negative event. As you don't focus on it, it doesn't grow. It dies of malnourishment and you are left with all the good. Bad times and tough events are part of life, so if anyone tells you that he/she can make your life thorn free, then they are biggest ….. as I don't want to give any power to them even by writing that word. When you learn and slowly master focusing on positivity you could go through rough/tough times with a smile.

Now the big question going in your mind is "how do I stay positive when things get rough/tough?" Because staying focused on the positive at times like this is the last thing on your mind, but it should be the first. Why is this that positive thinking is the last think on your mind? It is because you have mastered negativity, without any fault of yours. It has been given to you by the society and the system. There is loads of negativity around you, news channels are the biggest source of negativity on this planet. You now know that negativity is a learned behavior, so any learned behavior can be unlearned. You just need to focus on positivity now more than ever.

Practice is the key, as you mastered negativity unconsciously with practice. You can master staying positive by taking your mind off your problems and worries and re-energizing your mind. This is really important when you are having a bad day and you feel sorry for yourself and want to run away from everything. Initially it seems hard, but as you keep up with the practice this would become your second nature. You are building positivity muscle just like building muscle in the gym. It is a slow progress which is hardly invisible in the beginning, this is where most of you lose hope and stop muscle building. You are building mind muscle, focus muscle.

Below are the muscle building tips which would help you to build a regular practice, until the results are visible. This is a process, and, in this process, you might not notice the change because it is slow, progressive and you become the process yourself. Let's start the muscle building process.

1. Be very careful of who you hang out with, if you find yourself around those who are negative then break free from them. Because you are on a different journey now and negativity is like ---- disease which spread just by being there. It is just like climbing the mountain with looking backwards.

2. Put a cap on your TV hours, watch that is motivating and uplifting. Don't sit in front of the TV for hours, the news is depressing, mostly violence, death and negativity are shown on repeat. This activates negative and depressing emotions, making a cloud of gloominess around you. You

are forced to feel low and think as if there is no hope out there. They make you live a scared life. It keeps you away from the real beauty and wonderfulness of the world. They highlight few bad things and make you believe that the whole world had turned bad. If you do watch TV go for the more positive program such as a nature documentary showing the wonderful world in all its glory or a comedy.

3. Make your family your priority, your pillar. Try to spend as much time as you can with your family and loved ones. Discover somethings that you all can do together and which you all can enjoy. Aim to have one meal together every day if possible, otherwise accommodate one family night in a week where you can spend quality time together.

4. Make friends with books and motivational tapes (I think I'm still old school, so excuse me for using tapes). At a time when you feel particularly low and negativity begins to appear in life, listen to motivational tapes or repeat positive affirmations to regain a positive attitude. Best thing is to listen to some sort of motivation every day, it keeps the battery of positivity full all the time.

5. You have a dream, you like something, you want something, but are scared to follow that dream, admit that you like that something and you want that something. Responsibilities of life, family and this world have put permanent brakes on. You have one life; I'm not saying leave everything and just go crazy. But take time out each day to just do something that you enjoy, you dream of, just a little bit. In doing that you don't have to make choices or decisions, something from your heart which relaxes you to the fullest. Which makes you feel complete.

6. Exercise daily, when I say exercise daily it doesn't mean that you have to join an expensive gym and jump iron every day; and have tons of protein. You just have to get more active, you can take stairs instead of lifting few times a day when at work. If possible, go for a walk in the park and fill your lungs with fresh air. Touch a tree, hug a tree, talk to them, do what you feel like. Get out of your routine and break the cycle of "what would people say". Go swimming or join a hot yoga class, just move your body to circulate blood.

    You need to have a direction in your life, and that comes when you have a significant goal in life. Significant to you not anyone else. Mostly your dreams are not your dreams, they are the dreams given to you by your family.

This significant goal make you focus in one direction and save you from doing what you don't want to do. Break this goal in to steps and reward yourself when a step is completed.

7. Practice looking for good in all situations, especially in not-so-good ones. When things are not as expected, if you look hard enough, you may find that they are not as bad as they seem to be. Remember that the situation will not last forever, this is only a temporary stage that is going through and will improve.

Use affirmations throughout the day to instil self-confidence and positive thoughts and feelings. Learn techniques that allow you to get your attention and quickly focus on the task at hand.

Mind and Manifestation: The sky is your limit

Everything that we see that has been built by man, no matter how small or big it is was first conceived in human mind and then materialised. Your mind is a really powerful tool at your disposal, you could achieve anything you set your mind to. You just need to grow the wings of an idea because the sky is your limit. Once you have your idea than if you follow a few simple steps, you would be able to achieve anything in life. The most fundament rue to be successful is being absolutely committed to achieving what it is you want. You need to sharpen your focus and set your mind to that one goal. And finally take whatever steps are needed to achieve this. You have to approach this with conviction and maintain the focus, because if you lose focus you lose the idea. It won't manifest.

Let me share with you the story of Chinese bamboo tree. The seed of this Chinese bamboo tree is a hard nut to crack, it takes nearly five years to crack, before it even sprouts and come out of the ground. So, the story is that a farmer plated these Chinese bamboo seeds in his fields and every morning he used to go to the fields to nurture them. He would water them and put some fertilizers, did all the required process of cultivating. Few months passed by nothing came out of the ground, only the farmer knew how long it would take for his crop to grow. As the time passed, people in the village started making fun of him as they were not aware of what he had planted. Every morning they would walk past his fields and make fun of him. Time passed and after five years his plantation started to grow out of the ground and within six to seven weeks these bamboo plants grew sixty to seventy feet tall. Whole village was shocked and surprised.

The important question is, did it take plantation five years to grow or seven weeks to grow? Obviously, the answer is 5 years. The farmer nurtured his crop for five years every single day, because if he had missed one day the crop would have died.

You can grow 70 feet tall if you follow few relatively easy steps and nurture yourself everyday with them, make changes that are necessary to achieve what you want in life, let's learn the steps and grow 70 feet with the following steps.

Dedication and Devotion

According to Dictionary.com, dedication can be defined as "wholly committed to something, as to an ideal, political cause, or personal goal." When you say you are fully dedicated it means that you are wholly committed to that cause. In other words, it means being fully devoted to a thought, ideal, purpose, or goal. For example, you could be devoted to the ideal of a greener planet. Or, you may be dedicated to girl-education and fund-raising.

"The amount that you're willing to sacrifice is directly proportional to your desire for success." - Dan Gable

Sacrifice always goes hand in hand with dedication. For you to be successful in any walk of life, you must devote yourself to something you consider important. All successful athletes, actors, singers, artists, and writers had been fully dedicated to their craft and made enormous sacrifices before reaching the pinnacle of success.

You should take positive steps and decide exactly what you want to achieve in life and make it your goal/mission. Once you have decided what you want, you must do it with total conviction and commitment, just like the Chinese farmer. When you are planning and setting your goal, you must have the firm conviction that you will reach your goal.

Visualize

Visualization is a mental technique that uses your imagination to create what you want in life. When you use it in the right way, visualization can help you achieve success and prosperity, and improve your life. Your mind is very powerful, and visualization uses your mind to achieve success. We all use visualization in our lives, but we are unaware about it.

This is very common in athletes, especially high jumper and pole vaulters, all the superstar athletes have mastered this. When they close their eyes before the jump, you think they are praying, but along with prayer they envision their jump. They visualize in their mind a successful jump.

You should practice visualizing your goal from beginning to end and see yourself achieving the end result. This practice unifies your focus in the direction of your goal, and achievement of this goal becomes your subconscious mind's mission statement. Basically, to have reprogrammed your subconscious through visualization. Now it becomes easier to take necessary actions to achieve your goal.

Action Promptoo

The effect of motivation and visualization doesn't stay for long if you don't take immediate action. Once you have conceived an idea and had it properly visualized in your mind then next step is to take immediate and massive action. To make a permanent path for this new destination you need to keep walking again and again on the same path. Because if you don't action immediately there are chances that your new picture might fade away and you might even forget about it.

You know that taking the first step is the hardest part in the whole journey, once you have taken this first step things get momentum and your motivation increases. Now that you have reprogrammed your subconscious to take required actions in the direction of your goal. You are so customized to your comfort zone that this first step is like breaking the shekels. You are steeping into the unknow territory of uncertainty and doing what you have never done before take courage. Fear of uncertainty is good, but it should not hold you back from taking the necessary action. Because without action there is nothing.

There is a great buzz around the manifestation and law of attraction but visualization alone about your goal would never help to achieve it, taking action and continuous action is very integral part of the equation. When you say I'm committed to a certain task, it means nothing until you take the actions that would help you achieve it. Visualization is just one part of the equation, which has no meaning or power without action.

Don't change directions

Imagine yourself travelling from A to B with your best friend and he has got the map. After some time, he asks you to turn right and you do even though you know it is a wrong turn, then again after some time he asks turn left and you do the same. This goes on for some time and now you don't know where you are. And after covering few more miles you run out of petrol in the middle of nowhere.

This happens to most of us in daily life, you get an idea, set a goal and then start your journey, but the mistake you do is that you give the map to your mind. And mind loves best to stay in its comfort zone. You have to be very careful of all the distractions that come your way on this new journey in new direction. Even though you have practiced visualization, there are still strong chances of your mind taking comfort in old behaviour.

When you have made the commitment and have come to realize your dream or goal, you must have perseverance and be willing not to change your focus until you finally achieve the desired goal. Depending on what you set out to do, this could take some time, but it is essential that you stay as committed to the process as when it started, it could help you keep a diary of your project from start to finish, this way you can See how far you have come and keep your mind focused on the result you want to achieve.

Life has many unexpected peculiarities and could throw anything at us, so it is important that you continue pushing yourself towards the goal through any difficult time. Again, fear is the main problem and the main reason why most people do not achieve and renounce what they set out to do, if you give in to fear, you will only continue to put bigger obstacles in your path until finally I beat you and you give in. The sky is really your limit if you try to achieve it with perseverance and determination to overcome anything that crosses your path.

Rediscover your Creativity

You must have seen many people saying that I'm not creative, what saddens me the most when teachers and parents say this to the kids. Kids are the most creative, but the system and society takes that away from them. In order for them to be successful according to your definition and understanding of life, you put layers of expectations, responsibilities, cultures, good/bad, how/why and many more. And their creativity gets buried under these layers by the time they enter teens.

You have a creative side, which you might not be aware of. It is there and has always been there, but with time got buried. You only need to clear the layer that have accumulated on them. It might take some time in this clearing process as they have their unmoved for years. For some this can be quick and for some it would take some time, but it would surface for sure. You have to dig, practice and search for your creative side and bring it to the light. Here are few ideas which would help you in this rediscovery journey and give you back your creativity. Creativity is the key to happiness and higher self-esteem.

> **List:** take a piece of paper and pen and write down all the things you liked to do as a kid. It might take some time to remember all the things as it was a while back and those beautiful memories have been pushed to the back of your memory safe. Repeat this exercise for few days or even weeks, you would be surprised to see the things in this paper. The things which you have forgotten, the things that made you happy.

> Things that woke you up early on the Sunday morning. The things which made you forget food and water; you could do them all day without feeling tired.

Once you have completed the list, pick one thing that you enjoyed doing the most and start doing it at least once a week.

This formula is applicable in all walks of your life, where you feel there is a need of change. where you want to add new dimension of creativity. Just sit and start writing down the idea, try to add some flavour from the list of childhood favourite. You would notice feeling alive again doing this work. List down as many ideas as you possibly could for solutions and let your creativity flow.

Changes: you have to make some small and some big changes in life because they are necessary to clear the creative blockage. Creativity is directly associated with your right brain, so do activities to make this side of the brain more active.

There are so many simple things you can do every day, if you brush your teeth with right hand practice brushing them with left, start eating with left, writing with left. The bottom line is that do simple routine things with excitement and in a different way where possible. When you go for walk, take a different route. Shopping, go to a different store. You make these little changes to your daily life and get big channels of creativity flowing again.

Not so good ideas: we all are full of ideas some good

and some not so good. When you get a new idea, even if it is not so good and you think that it's not worth pursuing it; still pursue it. This would help you be creative and challenge this into a great idea. As there is nothing good or not so good, our beliefs make them good or great. Even if you only think of bad ideas, you are still creative, so work on the bad ones and develop them, whose saying that it is a bad idea anyway, could become a great idea and solution to your problems.

Accountability Buddy: when you work on new things out of your comfort zone, there are chances of getting complacent. That is why whenever you start on a new project, find an accountability buddy. This person should be one who you trust in and able to ask you questions. This motivates you to do the things which sometimes you don't want to do because you don't want to be embraced. This also help you finish things on time. You get some idea and feedback on how you are doing which act as check points. Brainstorming together is a great way to develop creativity.

Challenge yourself and others: if you challenge yourself by telling yourself you couldn't do something the way you always have done it; you will then have to think of new ways to get around the problem which could lead to some very creative suggestions.

Life coach: if you feel that your creativity is really exhausted, then consider hiring a life coach to help you find it, a life coach could help you establish the areas where your creativity is lacking and work with you to strengthen it. Life coach is not there to give ideas, his/her role is to make you aware of the layers that are covering your creative self and make you find your ways to uncover them. His role is just to guide (map) you, it's you who have to read the map and drive.

Become a child when it comes to imagination: put your adult brain to rest and let go of all your adult obligations, stresses, strains and worries and go back to your childhood. You were the most creative then, you had the best imagination and creativity which knew no bonds. You were fascinated by the dew on the grass, butterfly in fields, different shaped leaf or pebble on the ground. children have the best imaginations and their creativity knows no bounds, think like a child when you are stuck for creative ideas and they would soon flow freely once again.

Relax and Create: relaxation and creativity go hand in hand, more relaxed you are the more creative it gets for you. You could often become depleted of creative ideas if you are stressed, tired, burnout, depressed and unhappy. Relaxation comes to you from different sources, but the best relaxation is when you are at peace with yourself. There are many relaxation techniques, you need to try few and find what works for you the best. For me deep breathing is the one which brings clarity in my mind. Few deep breaths and all sorted, calm and relax. For you it could be walking, swimming or just having a cup of tea. Once you are relaxed and feel better, creativity flow begins.

Mind games: are simple games that challenge your mind and force you to think outside the box, analyses, calculate, design strategies and work with logic. Mind games challenge your mind and force you to think quickly and sharpen it and how it works. There are several mind games that can help you increase your IQ and creativity.

Word games are great for increasing your IQ. Games like Scrabble and crosswords stimulate the brain and expand the mind. Sudoku is another popular mind game that became very popular in the 1980sThis forces your mind to think logically and devise strategies to fill the grid successfully. The tests with riddles also stimulate your mind and make you think logically and analyse each part of the puzzle to arrive at the final answer.

Chess is another strategic mental game that forces you to calculate every move you make along with the consequences. You learn to perform multiple tasks and work with logic and strategy and solve problems to win the game.

Playing this kind of mind games increases your creativity because they work with your ability to think strategically and logically. A mind that is constantly stimulated to think from all angles and these mind games have worked miracles in lives of people, including children.

Creativity needs Shining

Creativity is not one that has to be imported from outside, you have abundance of it withing yourself, but it has lost its shine because you have forgotten to dust and shine it. When you begin to start cleaning your creativity and it begins to shine, it would benefit everybody. Whatever you see around you, is a creativity product of someone's mind. Once you begin to be more creative even in the small way, everybody around you would you're your creativity, in their lives. This could be used to help with projects, goal setting, home, family and a whole lot more. A bit of creativity brightens your life just like a candle do to dark room. For creativity to shine in your life, below are some tips, use few which you find interesting.

Stay Healthy

Find an exercise routine that you enjoy and stick to it. Change it when you want to but keep doing some sort of exercise. Sleep well. Eat a variety of healthy foods. Meditation or something you like to do to relax could help you keep your mind focused.

Explore New Things

We do so many things without thinking about them. These things become our daily routines – the mundane and boring. Try something new. It could be something as little as taking a different route to work or something like taking up a new class in something you have always wanted to learn.

Start Thinking Like Curious Mike

Ask yourself questions about everything you see, hear and read. Why? How? What if? Find out the answers to your questions. You could also keep a curious journal and track all of your findings.

Read a New Book

Choose one that you wouldn't normally choose. Pick one up at the library. If you have always preferred reading nonfiction, pick up a fiction book. There are so many interesting books to read and so many different genres to choose from. Your librarian would be happy to help you explore new books.

Act Like a Kid

Children are so carefree, honest and fun. Think about what you used to do for fun as a child. Paint a picture, take out those charcoals, get some finger-paints, go to your local amusement park…anything that a kid would do! And have fun!

Everyone Needs a Little "me" Time

Take some time every day to just relax. You could use meditation if you like to meditate. Don't make any plans, pay any bills...nothing. Just do nothing for a little while.

What If

What is the end of the world was tomorrow? What if you did go to college for business? What if aliens were real? What if there is an afterlife? Make up your own what if questions and just see where your brain takes you.

Never Assume Anything

Assuming anything always gets someone in trouble. You might assume that your boss is a jerk. What if he just doesn't like his life and takes it out on his employees? You might assume that the person who cut you off this morning was inconsiderate. What if they were rushing their child to the hospital?

Write About You

Who are you? What kind of person are you? Where have you been in your life? When are the most important things in your life? Why do you do things the way you do? How do you live your life each day?

Have Conversations with People

Listen closely to what they have to say instead of waiting for your turn to speak. What must it be like to be this person? Imagine how they live and think.

Intuition: Listen to your inner self

You all have intuition, it the little voice that comes from within us all the time. You listen to it or not depends on how tuned you are to hear this inner voice of yours. In the world of business, you are surrounded with internal noise. May it be your TV, iPod, traffic, or your colleagues at work. These days you don't the noise from outside sources, you create it for yourself. Every morning on my journey to London I see every person plugged to devices. There are few exceptions as always have been, but most of them not only listening to music but watching their favorite series. 7am in the morning, the time I don't even want to hear my own voice. I look at these long faces and think what they are going to be like by lunch time let alone in the evening. How productive they are at work?

I'm not against listening to music, but what music you listen matters because it affects your brain waves. Most of the music these days are higher Beta waves, which are the cause of stress in human doings. I used human doings because you have moved very far away from the status of human beings, which ones were pride of this planet.

We all respond to the events in our daily life in form of feelings and emotions, these events could be encouraging, discouraging, good or bad. You associate every event to an emotion and a corresponding feeling. You are living in a reactive state of being, therefore you react to every event, even those who have no importance and not worth of your time and emotion. Let's look at an example from our daily life. As I write this book, we are approaching Western festive period of Christmas, there is celebrations every day. When you put your dress on and look in the mirror, even before looking into the mirror you know if it's a hit or miss. If you like it there is a smile on your face and if not, then a shake of head. This is purely inner voice or what you call intuition. This is the simplest form of listening to your inner thoughts or intuition when it comes to making the best decision. This happens to you all the time, but you turn this little voice away with your logical reasoning.

We all have done this so many times and later realized that your inner voice was correct. But still you don't learn from it and keep on repeating the same mistake and then blame luck or others for the conditions of your life. I have done it several times, but I have learned from my mistakes and is very conscious of my little voice. Many times, getting into relationship, you had this feeling that it is not the right one, but you still went ahead to realise later.

However, if you make friends with your inner voice, you could use it to your advantage. Your inner thoughts could help you to succeed in life, become more confident and lead a happy, more fruitful and fulfilling life.

This perfect and wonderful instrument called body that you have to enjoy this life journey on this planet is the most valuable resource that you have at your disposal. It is there to serve you and it is your responsibility to make full use of it. Your intuition become stronger the better your relationship is with this body. It wouldn't let you down, because it is your best friend. You are its best friend or not depends on you. You have the basic intelligence to automatically know if something's right or wrong; and how to achieve the best by simply going along with your own intuition, and you know now that it doesn't let us down.

Making friends with your inner voice of intuition is rally easy and totally tricky at the same time. Together we will try to learn few ways to tap into our intuition and make friends with it.

Easy Choices:

Imagine you went out with friends to a restaurant which had buffet for dinner, different cuisines. You had your food and you know that your stomach is full, but you still long to try something else and you did try some more food. This is a typical scenario that you all face from time to time. Do you listen to your inner voice that is saying "stop, your stomach is full, don't eat any more?" No, you don't listen and stuff your stomach with extra food and later you suffer with so many things, you know them. But do you say, "I should not have eaten that much."

Yes, you shouldn't have eaten that much, your inner voice told you. Therefore, start off the easiest way developing your intuition by using it to make choices for less important decisions, examples could be, choosing what you want for dinner or which movie or restaurant to go to.

Sit with Self:

when you start this process of making friends with your inner voice, treat it like you would treat your new partner. You would make all the time to spend with them, would sit with them in a quite restaurant so that you can pay attention to every word they say. Similarly, when you start dating your inner voice, find a quiet room in the house and try to send loads of time with yourself. Some of my clients find it really hard to sit with themselves, they get scared by the thought of being alone.

I would admit that it sounds easy to be with yourself, but it could be really difficult because most of us have got thumb cancer (i.e. we are glued to our phones). You and I have forgot to live without them, I have seen people having panic attacks when they lose their phone for some reason.

But you can start even by spending 2 to 5 mins few times a day and then gradually increasing it. You would find it easier to tune into yourself and with your inner voice when it is quiet, so choose a room where you know you won't be disturbed when it comes to being on date with intuition. A good technique to use is to close your eyes and take a couple of deep breaths, focus entirely on the little voice and see what immediately comes to mind.

Admit mistakes:

You should be open to admitting that in this process of listening to your inner voice, you would make mistakes. You should be aware that intuition is always right, but your interpretation might to wrong. Therefore, trust the process, like any other process. When you start something new, you tend to make mistakes and same is the case with intuition.

Be willing to admit that you might make mistakes when listening to your intuition, while your intuition is usually right, you might misinterpret your inner voice that could lead to making a mistake. However, you should learn from the mistakes you make and continue developing and strengthening your inner voice.

No confusion:

 when letting your inner guidance come to your help, don't confuse matters by trying too hard or shifting the answer one way or another, chances are if you are inclined towards going in one direction then you already have the answer. But that is not the intuition speaking, it's your logical brain inn action.

Following the above is the easiest way to get your internal guide to start surfacing when you need it, the more you turn to it and use it, the easier it will be. As the cartoon character "Jiminy cricket" sang to his friend Pinocchio "he always lets conscience be your guide", the same applies in real life, follow your heart, your inner thoughts and feelings and you would never be wrong. It is only when we begin to lose faith and doubt ourselves that we become detached and undecided and this leads us in the wrong direction or in a stalemate.

Mental imagery works

One of the most powerful and inspirational tools which could be used daily is something which every one of us possesses, our very own imagination. Your own thoughts, insights, ideas and intuition could be used in your daily life to make positive changes for the better in any aspect of your life. Everyone has an imagination although some of us have a more vivid one that springs to life quicker than others do, but with a little practice, we could all form imagery in our mind to benefit us

Using the imagination as a tool

How you use your imagination to benefit you in your daily life is only limited by you, you could use your imagination to visualize any number of things and use it for almost any situation. Visualization works by forming a positive picture of the outcome of a situation and seeing this positive outcome in your mind as though it's happening and letting it replace any negative thoughts you had. You must develop the visualization as much as you could and look at it from all angles and perspectives, the mental picture which you build in your mind must be as clear as possible of how you wish the situation to turn out. Think of your imagination and the mental picture you build as a blueprint for developing and building on, just as an architect uses a blueprint when designing a project from start to finish.

The foundations

You need to begin with laying the foundations of your idea/goal or what it is that you want to change, in your mind and then gradually build up from the base. As discussed earlier very clearly visualize all minute nooks and crannies of the idea. Be very thorough about this as the foundation work involved in formulizing your idea would be the basis for your success. When you are formulizing the foundations ask yourself these few questions:

- What exactly do I want to achieve or change?
- What difference would this make?
- Could I achieve what I want on my own?
- What do I have to change in my life to achieve this?
- What should I learn to achieve this?

Once you have laid the groundwork for whatever you want achieve or to change in your life, then you can go ahead and develop your plan, visualize the project every step of the way as clearly as possible and see the project from beginning to end. in your mind as accurately as possible. When you have completed the visualization in your mind, then you could take steps to achieve what you want, if you wish, you could write down the steps you took in your mind in writing to achieve the result, and follow them from the beginning to finish.

The master points

The master points to achieve your goals in any aspect of life are:

- Focus your imagination on one idea. Remember "where focus goes, energy flows."

- Form as clear mental picture or image as you can of the idea and outcome in your mind. It has to be vivid.
- Have faith in your abilities and execute your plan with confidence.
- Follow the process with discipline till the goal is achieved.

Taking care of your mental health

Everything we discussed about till now have no significance if your mental and physical health are not in optimal state. It easier to check the status of your physical health, but mental or psychological health are bit hard to check. One major reason for mental health checks to be hard is that society has not accepted it as a condition like physical ailment which can be cured with proper help. Having a psychological condition still carries a big dogma around it. We are talking about living at Mars, but we still can't speak openly about our mental condition.

There has to be much more awareness and openness about mental health in society, in order to live a happier and healthier life as a community. There is a need for shift in the attitude towards mental health, you should take care of it at least in par with your physical health if not better. Both go hand in hand with each other, just like two wheels of the bicycle. If one goes flat you can't ride, and if you try then you damage the rim in the process and have to exert extra force. So, the focus should be in having both the wheels inflated to have a good ride.

One of the major culprits effecting your mental health is stress, and it has become the most common word in 21st century. Even I hear 6year old kids being stressed, this makes me really sad and you should also feel the same. If anyone thinks that 6year old being stressed is ok than that is also an issue. In a seminar few months back, I asked a kid no older than 7, "what is your favourite sports", he said "tennis". Then I asked him why it is his favourite, and to my shock he said, "because playing tennis helps me get rid of my stress". Everybody in the auditorium laughed expect me, because it is a serious matter and there is nothing in it to laugh about. This shows us the attitude of society in general about this issue. I can write a book on this subject (I think I will) but this introduction, just to bring to your notice the importance of this issue.

Where does this stress come from? There is a whole science behind how and why you get stressed but for simplicity I would talk about basic reasons. Firstly, I believe it has become a fashion in corporate world and in general to be busy and stressed. You ask anybody, 95% of the people would reply, either busy or stressed.

If somebody is not busy or stressed, they are considered under-performing. But in general life it enters our mind in many ways, it could be in the form of finances, job security, responsibilities, and even kids' homework. Cooking dinner and cleaning dishes have become stressful. For some relationships are taking their toll on their mental health.

Stress is one of the biggest factors in unsettling your mental health and ultimately your well-being, it is as important to reduce stress in your life, as it is to reduce your fat, sugar and calorie intake to remain healthy.

The internet is full of solutions for stress reduction, I believe that too much information is also the cause of stress. Searching about stress, stresses you. Below I have put together some suggestions that could help you reduce stress in your life.

- Stop the use of word STRESS in your life, eliminate it from your vocabulary. It would train your mind not to get stressed, because when you use the word stress, brain releases certain harmful chemicals in your body.

- Become a good at time management, rather than stress management. Learn to be smart with your day and time, set targets that are realistic and manageable.

- Focus on one task at a time as multi-tasking reduce your efficiency and increases stress. Stop juggling between tasks, just focus on one and then move on to the next one.

- Prioritize your work, make a list of all the task and the rate them according to their importance. And work on the important ones first.

- Flexibility is the key; you have to remain flexible in your mind when meeting deadlines. If you are not able to meet them, then don't beat yourself up for it. But don't make it a habit.

- Take small breaks throughout the day, these would give you time to clear your head and get back on track and stay focused on the task at hand.

- Raise your hand......Admit that you are only human, and you could not do everything, admit when you need a little help and don't be afraid to ask for that help should you need it'

- Learn when to say "no", while we all like to do favours we could sometimes take too much onto our plates and when this happens, we could not manage to fit everything in and stress sets in.

- Never try to overexert your body, you could only do so much in a day, by trying to push yourself continually beyond your limits would stress your body and mind.

- Learn to recognize when you are starting to get stressed and take immediate action to relieve that stress.

- Learn techniques which you could quickly eliminate stress, there are a wide range of techniques which you could use, with some working better than others and giving you better results. Techniques such as breathing exercises and visualization are very effective measure which could be used to quickly ease stress and let you refocus.

- Positive affirmations could help you deal with stress effectively, a positive mind with positive thoughts is a healthier mind and one to stress less eagerly.

- Always make time for some quiet time, time to just relax and do something you enjoy and don't feel guilty for taking this time out.

Killing ANTs
(Automatic Negative Thoughts)

Chapter 3

Killing ANTs
(Automatic Negative Thoughts)

Why do you have to stop negative thinking?
Why most people fail to stop negative automatic thoughts?

Automatic negative thoughts can cause serious damage to your confidence, self-esteem and your decision-making skills. They could prevent you from doing the things you always wanted to do and not saying what you want to say. And it is no secret that automatic negative thoughts would cause all kinds of problems in your life. Ranging from anxiety to depression, and considerably more in between. If you think incorrectly, your life experiences will also be negative.

There is a wide variety of knowledge on the Internet that covers the topic of automatic negative thinking and how it could consume you slowly. Most of you suffer from negativity from time to time and need to hear some negative thoughts to stay safe, but for some people it could dominate their lives so much that they feel totally uncomfortable in social situations. Not only am I talking about parties or going to a date, I mean tasks as mundane as shopping, going to a bank, going to a takeaway, just daily basic routines.

Do you think now is the time for you to change your life for the better or do you want to remain a shy, meek, insecure and low self-esteem person who doesn't really enjoy life? Someone who is constantly anxious to try to impress people and who is always worried if other people are doing right or wrong.

Or would you like to destroy those debilitating thoughts and become someone who can enter a room and people know immediately that they are there? Would you like to have a strong and secure presence so much that other people want to impress you?

Positive outlook

When you are positive, you can be motivated towards goals because you know within ourselves that we can succeed. When you are positive, we can live the life you want and empower us to achieve what you want to do. Most of the things that happen in your life are not luck; They happen because you have worked for them, either with a positive or negative attitude. Whatever you give in life, you will return.

"The positive thinker sees the invisible, feels the intangible and achieves the impossible."
Unknown author.

Those who have negative perspectives will probably be depressed, frustrated and sad. If he is determined that he can never succeed, that the pitfalls surround him and that the world is against him, he will be absolutely right. People with negative perspectives generally have problems with work, relationships and their health. An acquaintance of mine who is constantly in crisis, has many health problems and, although they are not serious, they give him more reasons to complain. He has difficulties with friends and family and has not established himself in a stable job for the past fifteen years. That is what negativity has done to your life.

With a positive outlook, life improves and doors of opportunity open. Those with positive attitudes have better health and greater longevity, and have better problem solving and coping skills. They create energy.

"Most people are as happy as they decide to be!" Abraham Lincoln

Fears and Phobias

Before we progress further let's learn what these two imaginary monsters are, that can cause so much of distress in your life. The fear is the one that is responsible for your fight or flight response. This enables you to react in case of a danger, animals have this same response to protect them from predators. A phobia is very similar to a fear, but it is much more specific when directing fear to a certain situation or object that causes discomfort in daily life. An example of some phobias is Acrophobia - Fear of itching or of the insects that cause itching, Achluophobia-Fear of the dark and Acrophobia-Fear of heights.

Before we look further into fear and phobias, let's see how phobias develop. There is no proper answer to how phobias develop. But studies show that they have their roots in childhood, mainly between the ages of 4 and 8. Typical example is of a child who gets sick and had to go to the hospital, and in there they are given many injections and had their blood taken for tests. In there they are scared and develop a phobia for blood and needles. This could eventually lead the child fear doctors and them refusing to visit GP (Doctor) when sick.

Fear and phobias are the biggest killer of your positive attitude. They are something that could affect you to some extent, while most of you could conquer your fears and most fears and phobias do not like you more than real phobias, for some people they fear and the phobia could be very distressing and have a high impact. Impact on your daily life.

Fear and phobias obviously cause negativity and constant negativity depresses you, while some phobias and fears could be profound, and you could break the control they have over you with time and help. There are several methods of help, and the more sown fear or phobia, the more likely it is that professional help is recommended in the form of therapy or hypnotherapy. If the fear is mild, you can overcome it using self-help methods.

Understand fears and phobias

In order to overcome fears and phobias, it is essential that you understand them, fear and phobia simply cause us uncomfortable thoughts and feelings when we place ourselves in certain situations. It can cause sensations such as nausea, vomiting, dizziness, a terrible sensation, strong pressure on the head, chest pains, a feeling of shortness of breath and trembling. These are all feelings that we allow ourselves to build and control our mind and body, dissipating fear is a matter of regaining control and putting things in perspective.

This is the basis to cure any form of fear or phobia, although if you suffered for many years it would take you longer to recover, recovery is possible. Phobias and fear are basically exaggerated anxiety and learning methods and ways of relaxing are a good start to cure fear and phobias. There are many self-help books, DVDs, courses and audio courses that could help you get started, any self-help material designed to treat anxiety and stress would help, but there are many aimed specifically at those who suffer from fear and phobia.

Benefits of overcoming the fear

The benefits of dealing with and overcoming the phobia and fear are immense and those who have recovered and overcome their fears and phobias have compared it to being reborn again, the world acquires a new meaning when the fears dissipate. A new positive perspective develops that leads to a happier and fuller life, you start to feel good about yourself and what you can achieve in life, you are finally free to do anything and everything your heart desires.

While occasionally there may be some anxiety for a while when you face your fear or phobia, it would be different from the intense fear that once disabled you. Once you have realized that the key to overcoming these feelings is within you, the fear you feel does not have the same control over you, once it did and eventually stop controlling you completely.

Overpowering Dissociation

Dissociation causes us problems with our emotions, physical sensations and how we feel about ourselves as well as the world around us. It is often associated with depression and anxiety or when a person has gone through a traumatic experience. People suffering from dissociation offer have feelings of unreality and often fear they are going insane or that they have some incurable illness. Talking with and being around others becomes almost impossible and deep anxiety that is caused by the feelings could develop into a social phobia.

The feeling of dissociation could vary from person to person depending on the circumstances that brought it about, but common thoughts and feelings associated with disassociation include:

- The world around feels unreal
- Not belonging in the world
- A grey fog covering their vision
- Like having a veil over your head
- The world is moving at a faster pace than normal
- Confusion
- A terrible feeling of not being able to cope
- Unsure of yourself

- Others find happiness but not you
- Extreme anxiety
- Feelings that everyone is against you
- Feelings that everyone is talking about you

These are just some of the feelings caused by disassociation and these feelings eventually cause the sufferer to believe that they have to turn deeper inward to themselves in order to get back into reality. They continually watch themselves for any brief glimpse that reality as they knew it is returning, of course the more they turn inward and worry the worse the symptoms are.

CBT (Cognitive Behavioral Therapy) could help those suffering to overcome feelings of dissociation particularly when the cause is severe trauma. Those suffering from dissociation due to anxiety and stress may be able to rid themselves of the feelings through self-help methods and the help and understanding of a doctor.

It is important to remember that the world hasn't actually changed, it is only your perception of the world and those around you that has really changed, and these are only temporary thoughts and feelings you are having. Once you have conquered and overcome what is causing the feelings of dissociation you would see things as you once used to. For those who suffer from feelings of dissociation due to depression and anxiety they should realize that the feelings are just that, no more than feelings and these feelings would leave in time. It is important not to be constantly studying them and wondering when they would go, try to accept that they are here for a time and give them no more thought. Once you have lost some interest in your feelings and are not constantly worrying about them it could be surprising how

quickly the world once again becomes the world you once knew. Accepting your feelings and any thoughts you might have during this period is essential, for it is only when you lose fear of the situation could you recover.

Doubt & Self-doubt

Does your self-doubt require examination? Is it preventing you from living rich, authentic and abundant life? Do you continually doubt your abilities? If the answer is yes to these two questions, then it requires a check. Most people are happy to never live for something. People store their emotions under the carpet in the hope that they would go away. But years later these emotions come to the surface in the form of addictions, illness, destructive relationships and behaviour.

Doubt and self-doubt are one of the biggest hurdles in having happy, smooth, blissful, content life and relationships. From my experience of life and as a Coach, these two are the major cause for breakdown of relationships and self-esteem. When these two enter into your mind they become your best of the enemies, they sabotage your happiness, confidence, trust and take you into a downward spiral. Doubt is not always bad; it could be helpful to a certain extend because you can blindly accept everything in your life. Understanding them is important to overcome them.

It is very easy to overcome doubt, if you don't doubt it, of course. You all live with a concept (misconception) in your heads that whenever you try anything new, you should be successful. It is a must for you to be successful in whatever you try. You all are in some way or form affected with doubt of some kind, small or big.

Let's look at science, do you think all the scientific advancement achieved would have been possible without questioning the prevailing assumptions at the beginning? Assume, you want to start a business or launch your book. Are you absolutely sure that it would succeed? When you start something, there would always be some fear or doubt at the starting.

Despite your doubt, you could not let it keep you from your ultimate goal. The reason is simple. You should face failure, in order to overcome doubt. There are hidden lessons in every failure which would be helpful in your success in the future, if you learn from it. Dive right into whatever it is without being making rash decisions. don't dive in without the right gear. You would analyse all of the possible consequences of your situation and you would embrace the outcome, whatever it may be. This is the secret to conquering doubt. You develop the courage to fight it and have self-belief of defeating it.

Belief is the destroyer of doubt, if you think that doubt is stopping you to achieve your goals and reach your full potential, you need to work on building your belief. Start with unlearning the doubt habit and begin to learn and think positivity and develop faith ability to be successful. Remember you will succeed if you think you would, and you would fail if you think that too. In this abundant universe, your thoughts are self-fulfilling prophecies so stop thinking negatively and practice positivity. Similarly, never pay attention to the people who discourage you, who enjoy planting doubts in you and who are in fact wolves in sheep's clothing. Make new friends, whose company lifts you up, who are full of life and their attitude towards life in general is positive and uplifting. People who always see the positive side of the things, those who don't know what is negative.

Now, you would be wondering whether these types of people exist in this world, because you see so much negativity around you. It is just like seeing few spots on a white canvas. You see the black spots but forgot that the rest of the canvas is still white. Similarly, world is full of positive uplifting people, who are there but we don't notice them. Once you start looking you will find them, believe me. I have found loads, since I started this new journey of self-discovery.

When failure strikes

Failure happens to all of us. There is no person on the face of earth who has never faced a failure in their life and you also are not fortunate enough to never experience failure in your life. All successful people in life have faced and overcome failure, there is no success without failure.

"The skill in success is learning from failure and embracing these experiences in a positive way."

You must understand that it is integral part of success and eventually your life. These would be times when failure fills your mind with doubt, and it would be hard to muster the confidence you built up earlier in the process. You shouldn't let go of your commitment, no matter how shaken you are by failure. In fact, all setbacks should simply prompt you to increase your resolve to make better attempt at accomplishing your goal. In order for this to materialize, you must train your mind to build self-esteem and self-confidence. Every step towards self-esteem helps get rid of doubt and you would be back to your successful ways once again.

Healthy doubt

Healthy doubt is the practice of questioning from a positive spirit, using constructive scepticism to reflect on the risks and pitfalls of the desire for the experience to be successful.

Doubt can hurt and help, since the usefulness of uncertainty varies depending on the circumstances. When you doubt that your loved ones or colleagues, who have your best interest in mind, you may unintentionally reject their advice or guidance. On the other hand, there could be people who would not give you a complete picture and your precaution could save you from making a wrong decision as a result of their recommendation. Therefore, you must strike a balance between your suspicions and your desire to believe that everyone has your best interest in mind.

The exercise of caution can help you avoid undue damage to your personal and professional life, but you can unintentionally close both people and opportunities, when you allow your suspicions to influence you extremely. Your intuition is a tool at your disposal when deciding if the person before you are telling the truth or hiding the facts.

Remember that some doubt can always be useful to gain wisdom or to move forward in life. But when it becomes a cause of your depression and inactivity or when it looks like an insurmountable obstacle on your way to your destination, take advantage of your energy reserves that could reinforce your mind. You have to strengthen your success to succeed at all costs and weaken the doubt by all possible means, so you can lead a life of satisfaction.

You can succeed because of your doubt or despite your doubt. Or you may have to accept the inevitable and commit to the worst-case scenario. If this happens, simply change the course, re-energize your cylinders and start again on your revised route. Defeat the doubt, before it defeats you.

It is wonderful to stay open to the possibilities and look on the bright side of things and life. I would like to share my most profound doubt; *"I doubt, if I exist?"*

Feelings of Helplessness

Do you feel helpless? Do you tell yourself that there is nothing you could do to overcome hurdles in your path and reach your goals?

You don't realize that today you are no longer helpless like when you were a baby. You wouldn't die if someone doesn't attend to you. You could feed yourself or call a friend when you need help.

However, many of you still react to the feeling of helplessness as if it were a life or death situation. Some would still do anything to avoid this feeling, such as shutting up their feelings with addictive behavior. How often have you found yourself grazing in front of the refrigerator, turning on the television, grabbing a cigarette without realizing that you were doing it? Often, this addictive behavior is a way to avoid the feeling of helplessness that can arise in an interaction with someone, or as a way to avoid the responsibility of taking care of their own feelings and needs.

The feeling of helplessness or being out of control in any situation is uncomfortable and can cause secondary feelings of stress, depression and anxiety. Helplessness is a fairly common behavior in abusive relationships. The abused individual believes that they have no power to change their lives, makes no attempt to get away from the situation. Children often show signs of impotence in if school. An example of frequent use refers to a child who performs poorly on math tests and homework may begin to feel that nothing he does will have any effect on his mathematical performance. If no intervention occurs, the child's feeling of helplessness in the face of any type of math-related task will be transferred to adulthood.

We all face feelings of helplessness to some degree or at some point in our lives, which is good as long as we get back on the right track and overcome these feelings. But for some, these affect their way of thinking and their lives. Here are some helpful tips to help you understand these feelings of helplessness and how to overcome them.

- You should start by identifying your fears, problems, issues and difficulties, which normally make you feel helpless and try to find the reason, the why; behind these.

- Build your support system that would encourage you on your journey of building new belief system so that you could become independent, self-confident and capable of dealing with anything that comes your way in the future.

- You could practice scenarios which make you feel helpless when you are in good mood. This would help you when this feeling of helplessness crops up. Similarly practice ways to deal with conflicts and problem, so that they could be easily solved when they arise.

- As you walk along this path of new self, you would get small success in the beginning. Don't ignore them, you have to
- acknowledge them, appreciate yourself and reward yourself in form of celebration. These small successes are the foundation of your successful goal.

- You need to be patience, as the whole change process could take some time, bit longer than you thought. Always keep your focus on the goal.

- If you have relapse and begin to doubt again remember that this is only normal and pick back up from where you left off.

- Perfection is a myth, always strive for improvement no perfection. Perfection is another cause for creating the feeling of helplessness, no one is perfect we all make mistakes.

- Major success would come your way when you identify what your needs are to develop the skills of self-coping, self-healing and self-confidence.

Helplessness is a major human problem in itself and it brings with it many others, the longer you keep it within you the more it grows making you feel that you have a lesser control over your life and the Goal you want to achieve seems out of site. You need to be aware of the symptoms of this invisible enemy of yours and below is a small list for you so that you could recognize them and kick them out of your life or even stop them from entering at very first place.

- When the feeling of defeat becomes your primary feeling; that is that you start to accept that no matter how hard you try or what you do, you would never be successful in life.

- When you start believing that you can't overcome your problems by yourself and become independent on others for help in overcoming every problem you face.

- When you surrender to inner voice that says to you all the time that you are incompetent. But introspect that is this your inner voice, or you have accepted the opinion of others?

- This is where you develop a fear so deep seated within you that very situation of life looks like climbing Mt Everest. You lose complete faith in your judgement in handling even daily tasks.

- When you are not your normal self for long and state of misery, unhappiness and anger become your natural self then that is a sign.

- When you think that the victim all the time and are in the need of reassurance and rescuer in all situations.

- When pessimism is your outlook for the life in general.

- When you begin to believe that others think of your as weak and frail.

- You become unhappy because you run out of people who are willing to look after you by solving your problems.

- The worst one is when you resign to the fact that you would forever be helpless and that you could not possibly change.

There are many ways in which you could help yourself overcome these feelings, the important thing is to remember that you are not alone and that you could regain control of your life and make important decisions to solve your problems successfully. All you need is to have faith in yourself and deepen your search within self and find that faith and bring it to the surface. While we all have the ability to overcome our problems ourselves, it is worth to receive advice from friends and family, as long as you do not rely on them completely to solve your problems for you.

Your Inner Conflicts

When you have a mind that is free from inner conflict you can experience inner peace and blissfulness. And the major advantage is that you would have a sense of clarity which helps you have a lot easier life. Your decision making becomes much easier and speed of reaching your goals increases. And all this is because you are not fighting an inner war, as all resources are working in one direction.

When you are fully committed to achieving your goal, life becomes much easier as distractions become less visible, it's not that they disappear but they notice them less. When you made a decision and stick to it, no matter what life throws at you, it helps your mind to focus and deal with all the obstacles in a clam and responsive way. Your inner conflicts could lead you in a nowhere land, where indecisiveness is dominant and you are inviting anxiety and stress with open door, by losing confidence in yourselves.

It is natural to have inner conflicts, we all have them in some shape of form during our journey, but it is important that you are able to recognise them and deal with them in an effective way. Quickly you resolve them, quickly you are able to move forward, bring your positive attitude back. By resolving your inner conflicts, you are able to build higher self-esteem, develop more focus, and are less stressed. You should listen to your inner voice and help it guide you when it comes to making choices and decisions. This would give you full control over your life and help you manage and achieve your goals that you have set in life. This would create a healthier, more relaxing and happier future.

When inner conflicts are dominant in your subconscious, they tend to mess around with your emotions and take you towards a life of low self-esteem, low self-confidence and sometimes depression; totally opposite to what you actually dream of. With this understanding, it becomes crucial to evict inner conflicts when they arise, and by not letting them take over.

This inner conflict could enter into your life through several desecrate doors, one major entry point is your indecisiveness or hidden feelings stemming from unsolved issues in your life, these could be the events from your childhood those had emotional effect on you but never came to surface. As mentioned earlier that, what you are as a person now, is the result of events that happened during your life. But as growing up you never dealt with them, instead you hide them under the carpet rather than facing and resolving them, as you never knew how to? You have to lift the carpet and sweep these hidden feeling and emotions out by addressing them on the merit they need. For you in championing unresolved issues and inner conflicts:

- You need to build trust in yourself, realise your inner potential and program your subconscious that you are capable of dealing with life and it's situations by yourself and become the person that you dream of becoming.

- Your life is sum total of where you have focused your energy, so learn to focus on things that you want to achieve and centre it on yourself, notice what are the causes of distraction and develop plan to avoid them.

- You are on a journey, if you want to travel far without getting tired, make your backpack lighter by letting go of the feelings and thoughts you have harboured from the past. You can't win a race looking backwards. Let go of the past, old beliefs that are not yours, old habits which are not helpful, emotions that have held you back.

- Practice visualizing the new you, the more confident you and the peaceful you until it manifests in reality.

As you all know that there is no magical pill to have that could make inner conflict disappear without any effort. Like in any other walk of like, this would also need practice and time to resolve this issue and to begin build an inner self without inner conflicts. However, there is no magical cure and it would take time to resolve these issues and start seeing a better way of dealing and coping with life. The key point is that could change and only you could force this change within yourself, no matter which path you choose. In the end it all basically comes down to the common solution and that is change your feeling and internal dialogue to resolve your inner conflict and have a peaceful life.

Intimidation

Have you ever wondered, why 10 years ago almost every top-notch golfer would fall apart on the final day, when paired with Tiger Woods? Why would that happen so often and to the best golfers? Why were they intimidated or what did Tiger do to intimidate them?

Many psychology experts call it, "Tiger's eye!" He must have mastered the art of intimidation, but my thought on this is that his presence and success intimidated opponents. There have been several studies on how his presence intimidated other players.

Using brute force is not the only way to intimidate others, you could intimidate them in a very delicate way. It could be the way you dress, the way you talk, your position in society, the titles that you or your friends have. Most of the time the assumptions you make about others are simply untrue. You on autopilot think that they are "above" you and they don't like you, or so many other things. Your thoughts are based on assumptions that you don't justify, and all of these assumptions get in the way of you connecting with them confidently and even creating relations that could eventually benefit both parties.

You could face intimidation anywhere in life as it has been part of the human society since the beginning. You will encounter it in all walks of life if you have lower self-esteem, and also it could hit people at any age. This intimidation to some extends can be compared with bullying. Most of you are normally unaware of being intimidating, and on the opposite side, for some it this could make life/work/school difficult on daily basis. There are also chances that you are an intimidation to others, and you are not aware of it.

This sets into your subconscious from the early childhood as you are thought to fear people with power, like teachers and police were the most common. For you to free yourselves from this you need to catch it, check it and then make an appropriate change. you need to understand the difference, if the other person has a gun then definitely "YES", but if he/she is a senior executive then it is a big "NO". In order to win the battle with intimidation you must have a clear understanding of what intimidation is, it could come with many masks.

- If someone uses force/power to get what they want from you.

- If others threaten or use power to get what they want from you.

- Making you believe that they are more powerful than you.

- If your boss, teacher or partner hold punishment over your head of being fired, detention or divorce respectively.
- If they are being quick tempered, angry or getting into a rage with you, to get you do what they want.
- If someone uses their wealth to get you and others to do what they want.
- If they use ethnic or sexual insults towards you and others.

Now that you have understood the masks, it is time to face the situation/person and stop them from intimidating you. The very first step that you should take is to evaluate yourself and determine if your irrational, unhealthy way of thinking has allowed yourself to become intimidated by others. If your answer is yes, then consider taking following steps:

- Practice fresh and better ways of thinking that could help you conquer and respond to the intimidating people.

- Showcase your new ways of thinking and acting to those who have been intimidating you, this would the message to them that you are no longer intimidated by them.

- Plan in advance the ways to deal with people, in case they respond negatively to your new self.

- See the consequences of your new assertive behavior.

- Stick to your plan and accept whatever the consequences are of your new behavior.

When you start implementing this strategy of new self-belief, there would be the times of uncertainty or unsurety in your new methods. Therefor you have to keep on the discipline and reinforce these new beliefs till they become your second nature. For me daily positive affirmations and self-talk do the trick whenever I have to incorporate new habit in my life. Few of my positive self-talk are,

- I carry the power to change withing me.
- I'm on a journey and self-love is my fuel.
- This my life and I'm commander of my ship.
- I would keep walking on my path to success, no matter what.
- I'm my best friend and the only rescuer.

Trauma

Trauma is a life-threatening experience outside of normal human experience and this is one of the major problems that you might have experienced in childhood and teens, but this is mostly hidden in plain sight. When this goes untreated, it results in unhealthy and self-destructive choices in later stages of your life. This trauma could have been in any form; physical, verbal or sexual abuse. Bring told again and again that you are worthless and would amount for nothing in your life. This is not always easy to recognize that your difficulties in life are the result of some traumatic event.

The situation becomes more difficult as you are unable to trust others and do not share your true feelings or experiences. As there are several thoughts and emotions attached to these traumatic experiences which you are unaware of. You tend to mentally block this experience or might try to relive it again. Many people who are recovering from a traumatic experience mentally block out the experience that caused distress while others would relive it time and time again. Trauma could bring feeling of shock, disbelief, denial, emotional pain, anger, blame, sadness and in many case anxiety and depression.

All of the above are the most common feelings and thoughts associated with having gone through trauma; these feelings could come in no particular order and at any time. What you should realize is that these feelings are only natural and are your body and minds way of coping with what happened, the feelings and thoughts would eventually dissipate with time. There are many ways you could cope with them and help yourself to overcome them, the best way for you of course would depend on the severity of the trauma you were exposed to. There are however a number of coping skills which could be learnt in order to help you overcome trauma.

Self-Image

Chapter 4

Having an Optimistic Self-Image

Self-esteem is how you feel about yourself, but self-image is how you see yourself and how you think others see you. These two are closely interconnected because if you have a poor self-image of yourself or lowly opinion of yourself, it is definite that your self-esteem would be low.

As this book is about your self-esteem and it would be unfair not to mention self-image as these two are interrelated. To do justice to this subject, in this chapter we will discuss self-image and its importance in achieving goals of your life.

In simple terms self-image is the way you see yourself in your mind. These are the internal images, pictures, sounds and feelings of yourselves that you recognize as 'you'. It could be how you look in the flesh or your opinion about who and what you are (self-concept). It is very important as it has direct affect your confidence and self-esteem. Your self-image is really powerful because it would never deviate from your internal image. Your mind behaves in a manner consistently with the type of person you think you are.

The self-image is to do with your perception. Therefore, the way you look at yourself is vital because this would affect your behavior, thought process and your social relationships. You respond to events in your life positively or negatively according to your confidence. Your trust in relationships depends on the self-image you have of yourself.

Many of you are not aware of your own image until you really look! Usually, you are engrossed with the images that are bombarded every day by the media and the people around you, and you are left with to time to examine yours.

Self-image

How you see yourself goes a long way to how you feel about yourself and how others see you and think of you. If you think positively on the inside, then you would glow with confidence on the outside and come across this way to others. Feeling good about yourself is essential if you are to be happy in life and make the most out of life, it could make the difference of you being successful or failing, it is all about how you see your self-image.

People suffer from low self-esteem for many reasons and if they have been brought up feeling negatively about themselves then developing a positive self-image would be difficult, but not impossible. Developing a positive outlook is about changing your thoughts and feelings about yourself and if you have been thinking negative thoughts for a long time changing the habit would take time. However, by adapting a new way of thinking and sticking to this new way of thinking you would eventually banish unwanted negative feelings and would automatically replace them with positive ones in your day to day life. When this happens your outlook changes and with your outlook, you change, where once you might have thought something would be beyond your capabilities you would now look at it in a different light and begin to realize it is within your grasp.

There are many ways which you could use to develop a more positive self-image and esteem, there are self-help books dedicated to the subject, audio sessions which you listen and follow, DVDS, hypnotherapy audio or attending counselling sessions. They all however rely basically on the same principle, understanding what confidence really is, gaining confidence in yourself, ridding yourself of negative beliefs and replacing them with positive ones and learning strategies which allow you to remain confident in any situation.

The basics behind developing a more positive outlook and self-image are

- We all have our own definitions of everything in our life, to have different one for self-image; you have to start with thinking about positive self-image and confidence. And most importantly understanding this would mean to you.

- Since we were born till date, we have been taught to learn about everything other than us. We never had the opportunity to learn about ourselves. Wouldn't it be great to know ourselves better, understand our weaknesses and strengths, try to work on our weaknesses and build on our strengths?

- Negativity is a big part of the society and we have big influence of this in our lives. We need to move away from this negative culture by bringing in positivity in our attitude and thoughts.

- As we have learned many things till now that would help us on this journey of change, reflecting on what we have learnt and seeing the positive changes we are making to our life would encourage us to keep walking.

Self-talk is one of the major parts of convo, we all do it all the time, sometimes consciously but mostly unconsciously. We get between 60,000 to 90,000 thousand thoughts per day, most are repetitive and negative. This makes a major chunk of our self-talk and if you notice carefully most of the time you are continually putting yourselves down and there is very little self-appreciation in all this psycho drama that goes inside your mind. This has to be stopped and changed. You are on journey and want to change unhelpful self-talk by replacing it with positive self-talk, the easiest way to do this is by

- Watching your thoughts as they enter your mind, get rid of irrationals and replace them with rational ones.

- Replacing negative thoughts and feelings with positive.

- Begin to appreciate and credit yourself for the smallest of your achievements.

- As said so many times earlier, make positive affirmations your best friend.

Self-Image Transformation

As in this fast-paced life of 21st century, you are very much focused on the physical outlook and place high importance to eating healthy, exercising and dieting. You are spending loads of money on organic, vegan, ketone and many other types of healthy foods. But in the business of keeping the physical body healthy most of you don't realize that working on your self-image is just as important as working in the gym or hot yoga class. You have to maintain the balance between the two to have a healthy lifestyle. You must allocate time for yourself to understand how you feel and think about yourself, as this goes a long way in bringing content, happiness and success into your life. In order to build a healthy self-image, you have to do a mind workout as you do physical workout for your body.

In every journey the most important thing is the destination, if there is no destination there is no journey. Similarly, when working on your self-image, every first step you need to take is to decide what exactly you would like to be and secondly do an inventory of things that you are good at and love doing. There is no right or wrong answer, you could say that you are good at tennis, painting or even spending time with friends, but the only thing you don't want to do is to create a list of things that you don't like about yourself. You don't create this list of unwanted things which you want to improve upon, because these would only make you feel inadequate and hinder your journey to change yourself and your self-image. By focusing on the good in yourself and working on the limitations, you would be able to change your self-image into the one that you have been dreaming of.

Visualization and affirmations are every big part of this journey as they work as lubricant to the vehicle of life and play a very important role in making you realise how good you and your life already is. Like I always say in my seminars, "if you are still breathing, you still have the power to change anything in your life". Visualization has immense power, so imagine yourself doing and becoming all that you originally dreamt of and repeat positive affirmations through the day, this would help the new way of thinking sink in. By vividly imagining this new you, your mind would help you keep the focus on your goal, and this become catalyst in your journey.

Journaling

This is one of the things which I ask all my students to do from the very first of our coaching journey. I can't impress upon the benefits of keeping the journal and writing the process again and again. Some of my students have started writing gratitude journal on the very first day and a still doing it years after they achieved the results they wanted. They feel pride in doing that and sometimes send me pics of their journal and the journals of their kids or partners, which is every heart-warming.

You could start journaling about anything, I tell kids to journal about their school, dance classes, or simply their whole day. But when keeping the journal, you have to be very clear what it is about and why you are writing. This would give a different approach to your writing; you would be focused on more relevant things rather than filling it in with all unnecessary things.

As in this book we are working on building your self-esteem, I would recommend buying a self-esteem journal, buy one of Amazon or eBay (you can write on your iPad or computer if you are the one who want to save the planet). Where you buy from is not important, but you develop a habit of writing daily is important because in this journey you would really benefit from keeping a journal about your progress, you would be able to track the progress. You would be able to look back and see if you are keeping up with the schedule. This would massively improve your self-image and reinforce the new you. It is important that you track your progress as this would help you stay focused and as you know focus is the key to unlock all the locks of your life. This process would help you develop your new self-image at speed because you are fully focused on what you are achieving and what speed you need to work with.

Basically, if you don't keep track of goals and the progress, they would evaporate in the business of life because you are programmed to work on the things that are in your comfort zone. You are scared to move out of this zone of yours to the unknown, which most people scary. But when you start putting things on paper, you are training your mind to walk in a different direction, this could be the first but the most important step. Just like typing the destination in the GPS.

So, the power to keep written notes should never be underestimated, there are many ways in which they can help you achieve better success in life. You can use it to help you connect your feelings and thoughts, and this is the most important thing that you succeed in life. Your journal could help you discover what motivates you in life, develop new skills, learn new strategies for dealing with life in general, write and plan ideas and learn more about the person asking questions about you and writing answers to those questions. The journal is an essential tool when it comes to learning about yourselves and if you are to succeed in life and knowing yourselves is very essential. While you may think you know, but very few of you do. By keeping a journal, you begin to realise all the little things you don't really know or understand.

Keeping a journal is essential because idea or ideas could appear at any time, and some of the best inventors and thinkers have kept diaries, including one of the most prolific inventors in history, Thomas Edison. One of the most useful things a journal does is giving you the ability to review and consult records, for example, if you encounter a problem and have overcome it in the past and a similar problem has arisen, you could refer back for the solution and apply it or adapt it to a more positive outcome. Your journal could remind you of past achievements, which greatly contributes to developing self-image and helping you succeed in life when things get tough.

Goals

Food for thought: you know why most people don't succeed in life? Not because they don't have goals, but the goals they have are too small and mostly irrelevant to what they actually are. To be successful in life and to maintain a higher self-image you must have bigger goals. The goals that could stretch you, keep you awake whole night without feeling tired, make you jump out of bed without the help of alarm clock, you are buzzing whole day, without 5 cups of coffee in your system. Dream big to achieve big, to have a life of purpose, a life of contribution.

You are on a journey in this life, don't be stagnant. Everything around you and within you is changing every second, millions of stars dying as are the cells in your body, start you see at night might have died 100 light years ago and all your body cells are replaced approximately every seven years. Having a goal that would stretch you, could help yourself grow a positive self-image. If you set BIG goal for yourself and then go all-out to reach it, giving yourself something to work towards everyday creates success in your life – which is a vital part in reshaping your self-image. You could set smaller goals in line with the bigger goal in different areas of your life; work, personal, health, relationships, fitness, because it is not to ignore other areas of your life when working on achieving BIG goals. There is no goal without a completion date, if you don't have a date next to your goal it is just a dream that you wish of coming true one day. Therefor it is very important to set yourself a genuine time frame to accomplish each goal on this journey to achieve your ultimate life goal. And never forget to appreciate yourself and celebrate your success.

The path you choose to change your self-image is your personal choice, there are several paths that you could take and there are no limitations on what you could achieve if you set your mind (focus/concentration) to it. You should be fully committed and determined to work towards achieving the desired goal. There would be times on this journey when you would feel that there is no light at the end of the tunnel, the picture you painted of your goal becomes blurry and mind is full of doubts, don't get scared this happens to all who strive for bigger goals. It is absolutely normal, but do not let these put you off and discourage you. When this happens, sit back and have a deep breath, regroup your energies and get back on track working with same determination as before.

When you set a goal, you are committing yourself to working hard to achieve what you want. Once the goal is set with a completion date, you should plan a PLAN to achieve this goal of yours. "Most people don't fail because they plan, they fail because they fail to plan."

One thing that I would want to add to this process is ask yourself a question, "why I want to achieve this goal?" you need to be very cleat of this why in the whole process, because this "why" would keep you going when the going gets tough. Make a list of your Why's, frame them and always keep them in visible space.

Learn from the past

A technique which is very popular and one which keeping a journal could help you accomplish is the "best-better" technique, this technique could be applied to any situation that crops up in life and simply relies on you looking back on the situation and finding what you liked about it or what you experienced from it and then deciding how you could do better next time or how you could have better experienced from it. The key to recovering from past mistakes and succeeding in the future is to learn from your mistakes but remember to focus on your strong points

108

rather than your weak ones. If you concentrate more on your weak points rather than your strong ones, then very often this leads to you unconsciously reinforcing them which then lead to low self-esteem and of course having a low self-esteem isn't positive. It is only by building on your strengths could you increase your self-esteem and your self-esteem is the crucial factor to understanding your weaknesses and correcting them and therefore building a positive outlook on life which greatly increases your chances of success. So, by noting down your experiences in your journal you are able to look back on them and gain a clearer understanding of yourself and how you feel which ultimately determines how you think and how you think determines how successful you are in life.

Sooner the Better: Combating Low Self-Esteem

Many experts have provided various theories on this subject of self-image, ranging from human chemical imbalance to lack of faith, opportunities, discipline and many more. Most of them agree, that the number one cause of low self-esteem is lack of love, support, encouragement and positive feedback given to you during early childhood years.

The most common and influential reason for this feeling of insecure childhood is, when people become parents while they themselves are not mature enough to handle their own problems.

They are still coming in terms with their adulthood, responsibility of a partner, and they have no focus on family and family responsibilities. The high living standards that you want to live have made both parents work long hours, while coming in terms with real world. You are in a race to be better than your friend, cousin or partner, some of you are trying to prove yourself to your demanding parents. In the mist of all this happening in your life, your children get neglected, and you don't even know about it.

I meet several people in the late 40's or early 50's, who admit that in winning the race of life they lost their kids, accumulated all the material wealth but lost the priceless possessions. And the condition of the parents of X-gens is even worst, they are facing the war with social media, as they are addicted themselves and their new-born babies get this addiction as early as the age of six months. We are losing the work life balance to maintain a lifestyle that we don't even know that we want, we just want things because others have them.

Sometimes it's too late to understand that you are just following the footsteps of your parents and imposing same restrictions, pressure, expectations, but somewhere deep down inside you expect them to behave the way you wanted to behave against that behaviour of your parents. People get confused in their own minds, as they are not clear of what they should expect of their kids. Because they could not do it, this is not right for the kid. For example, many people would not let the kids do what they themselves were not allowed to do, irrespective of kids' talent. You force your definition of failures in life on your kids, without understanding that your kids are different from you and have

110

different potential. People should be sincere in giving advice, and in complimenting kids when appropriate. You should not ignore the efforts of kids as they are learning to accommodate themselves in this tough world.

One more important factor is that when you were children, you truly believed in your hearts that every adult is right and epically your parents. You always believed as kids that their values and feedbacks are correct. However, to your surprise too many of these adults raising kids are still fighting their own battles like drug abuse, gambling, alcohol abuse and other very social issues.

The bottom line is that most of the adults are basically not doing what is best, either for themselves or for their children, especially with the that their kids would follow their footsteps. People with addiction does not see the harmful physical, emotional and psychological abuse passed to their children as they get and stay too hooked up in their own spotlight.

In short, children and adults of all ages do need positive feedback and people to demonstrate in a sincere manner their care and concern. Start-up young and encourage your mate and children to make good, healthy, positive choices. And when they fail at something offer them hope and encouragement to try and try again.

When you become parents and even before you become parents, you should develop self-understanding and positive self-image, check for hidden emotions or traumas, check for goals and aspirations. I would love to see in my lifetime, a global emotional well-being test for the parents across the world before they bring a life to this planet. That "sooner" is what I want the preparation to root back. Don't be a parent for the sake of being a parent, like what happen with Asian couples.

To drive a car, you need a driving license; when buying a house your bank checks your financial record; in a job, company check your qualification and experience. When these minor things need some sort of validation, test and experience, then when it comes to an infinitely valuable life, why there is no check on the planet?

Self-Worth

In this world everything has a worth and if something is worthless you tend to not have it. But when it comes to your self-worth, you often use the phrase "I'm worthless", How could you do that? You are the most valuable and sophisticated life on this planet. The self-worth we are talking about is not the money you have in the bank, the million-pound house you live in, or the number of expensive watches; this is what you value yourself as a human life. You have to understand and build in your belief system that you are the most valuable thing you could ever have. Your self-worth is what you think you are, therefore never underestimate your self-worth, self-worth is all about price tag you give yourself. If you think you are rich in confidence then you would carry it around with pride, and if you think you are

112

poor in confidence then you would be hiding. Whatever valuation you give would be visible to the outside world. When you come to understand that your self-worth is independent of external valuation, then you would be able to face the face of life with greater confidence and would have optimism about the future. You are more likely to be able to reach your goals and gain experience, content and happiness from life. You would be able to build lasting relationships that work and are better copiable with whatever life throws at them. Higher the self-worth, higher the self-esteem and more happier you are. You begin to possess the ability to cope with anything and anyone throughout your life and are capable of doing anything you set your mind on doing or achieving.

Undervaluing your Self-worth

You will face several problems in your life if you undervalue anything, may be your car, house, job. In similar way many problems come to surface when you underestimate your self-worth, when everything else in life is overvalued. There is big inter-relation between self-worth, self-image and ultimately self-esteem, many problems would occur in your life simply by underestimating your own self-worth. Your lack of self-worth has impact on your sense of wellbeing, your feelings and needs, affects your ability to make healthy choices in relationships, work and life; and also cause fears such as rejection, neglect or abandonment. Similar to self-image, the lack of self-worth has been attributed to being indecisive, addictions such as smoking, drinking, drug abuse, compulsive shopping disorder and problems with eating such as anorexia.

Realizing your self-worth

All of us are capable of realizing our self-worth, we do not have to do anything special in order to be worthy of higher self-worth. The basic fundamental rule to realise your self-worth is that you stop the little voice (self-talk) in your head from putting you down all the time, your own stories, thoughts and feelings are what creates your self-worth. Your self-talk has developed over a long period of time and had casted a belief of self-doubt onto yourselves. It has genuinely made you believe that you are not valuable or capable, and thus in your own minds you develop undervalued self-worth, not some outside force creates it.

Your self-talk or thinking pattern could be changed in several ways, which could help you to boost your self-esteem that in turn begins the process of recognizing your true self-worth, the fundamentals behind making these corrections are that:

- You need to learn to recognize self-critical thoughts and change them the uplifting ones.

- You need to learn to replace negative self-talk with more positive one.

- The above two steps would be of no use until you make them a habit, you have to stick to the process of this change till it becomes your second nature.

There are many ways in which you could begin to set the pattern of changed thoughts but perhaps the best and the simplest one is using positive affirmations; few examples of positive affirmations could be:

- This is a new and exciting challenge – this could be used to replace thoughts such as this is too hard, or I couldn't do this it's beyond me.

- I am a confident and worthy individual – use this when you have thoughts such as could I do this, or I could never do this.

- I could do anything my heart desires if I put my mind to it – use this to replace thoughts such as I'm not sure if I'm qualified of completing this task or I don't know if I could complete what is asked of me.

All of these simple affirmations that you could use, gradually change the way you think, which in time would change the way you feel about yourself and encourage you to realise your real self-worth.

Developing your full potential

*"Every creature is trying to grow to their full potential on this planet (*or/and others, if they do exist somewhere else in this universe*). Tree is trying to be a full-fledged tree, dog is trying to be a dog, earthworm is just trying to be an earthworm and nothing else, they strive to be in this existence at their full potential."* Sadhguru

But the question that bothers me a lot and I think would make to think is, why do humans not strive to be full-fledged humans?

There could be many reasons and answers to this question; it is my humble request to every human that you ask yourself this question and give yourself time to reflect upon it.

Going back millions of years to the beginning of human evolution we humans were not the strongest of the creatures when lived in jungle (we still are not), so we learnt to fight or run and became fighter. Later we felt the need for shelter, we built houses in caves and some made caves by cutting stones and we became builders out of our requirement for safe place. And this evolution continued, and we kept on learning new skills in this process of better living and safety. Then came the cars, planes and rockets, along with radio, cassette player, TV and satellite channels. Not to forget phones, iPhone, internet and social media.

These all were supposed to be our assistants or in strong words our servants, but these were cleverer than us and they made us their slaves. We human fools still think we are the bosses and these trade/inventions are our servants, but the reality is that with all these in and around us, we have forgotten the real human in us; who is free from anxiety, jealousy, judgment, fear, anger and full of love, happiness, content, trust, blissfulness.

Most of you pretend to be happy in life by achieving small and insignificant accomplishments in your life, the reason I said insignificant is because if you develop the attitude of pushing further and achieving higher goals; then only you would be able to realise your full potential. It's not much you have to push; it is just a little bit that would make massive difference. There are several things that you might be good at, but you never tried, just got stuck to one thing, that is why you could never find your true passion. Develop the courage and belief in yourself to live life of passion.

When children, you were full of passion and brilliant ideas, which never stop flowing because you had an open mind and full belief in yourselves that you could achieve anything. But as you grew up the fear of "am I doing the right thing?" and of speaking out and being mocked took over. These internal thoughts stopped the flow of your imagination and ideas. You held back your thoughts and this stopped you from developing your full potential.

There are many ways you could start developing your potential, it's never too late. You should remember that there is no right and wrong way of thinking and many times the reason why others try to make you feel inferior when you voice opinions and ideas is because they wish they had had the idea and courage to speak up. You need to start focusing on your skills and abilities, and let your imagination and thoughts run free, trust them to genuinely excel in life.

All successful people have made mistakes in their journey and you should understand that making mistakes is part of life, no one is perfect. When you try and make mistakes, this is absolutely fine as these mistakes provide you acknowledge, and you should learn from them. There are certain qualities that you could cultivate for developing your real and full potential are;

- Working hard – putting your all into everything you do when working towards what you want in life.

- Having patience – things don't happen overnight so have patience and you would be rewarded.

- Determination – stick to your guns and never give in when things don't go your way, or you come across hurdles.

- Commitment – be committed towards your goals and what you what to achieve, set goals in mind and don't let anything or anyone stand in your way of reaching them.

- Organizational skills – the more organized you are the easier the road to success would be, plan out your ideas to their fullest before putting them into action.

- Learn from mistakes – you would make mistakes along the way, but you could learn valuable lessons from these and move on.

- Confidence in yourself – you have to be self-confident and believe in yourself and your ideas, there is no room for doubt.

- Stay realistic – don't set yourself goals that you could not realistically achieve in a set amount of time, by setting yourself unrealistic goals you are setting yourself up for failure again and again.

On the journey of developing your full potential, the two most important things to consider are, what you want out of life (specific goal) and what you could realistically (action) do to make that possible. Once you have these two, then you could go full steam ahead towards achieving what you want.

Run and Boost your Self-Esteem

Setting a new goal and taking steps towards achieving it is always good for boosting your self-esteem. Running has been a big part of this journey for many people, as it has many positive effects on your life like better physical fitness, stress-free life and most importantly higher self-esteem. This could be a wonderful and great self-esteem booster, especially if you have never done running before and had the belief that you could never run a certain distance (e.g. 10K OR 20K). This would help you to test and expand your limits like never before and with each landmark you reach you would find yourself more confident and able to take on the world.

Slow and Steady wins the Race

If you are like me who could not run to the letterbox at the end of your street without huffing and puffing, then definitely you should set a goal to run. Set small daily milestones to accomplish so that you are able to achieve them and by completing them you should feel a great sense of pride and accomplishment in yourself. The first time you go out, it's not that you have to all the distance running, you could probably do the combination of walking and running. However, if you discipline yourself to follow the plan, you will slowly start running more distance every day, and eventually one day you would be running the whole distance without stopping.

The most important thing to keep in mind is that you start out slow and try not to overdo things in the beginning. As your muscles would need some time to adjust to this new active lifestyle, and especially if till date you had an inactive life.

When you overdo in the beginning and injure yourself, that could be a big discouragement, particularly after seeing the progress that you made. As you know that we all are different and our physical capabilities are also different, some of you would love to increase your weekly mileage not more than 10%. Listen to your body and do what works best for you, some of you could handle a big mileage increase and some would need to increase their mileage much more slowly.

More psychological than physical (90% mental)

"I can do it, or I can't do it." You are absolutely correct in both instances.

Your brain muscle plays very important part in any your life, developing psychological muscle is as important as developing physical muscles. It is believed that achieving any goal, depends 90% on your mental capacity of conceiving the idea of the goal achievement and penetrating this idea into your subconscious mind. You could do this and build this in your brain, simply by telling yourself "I could do it; I could finish the race, I could run for 30 minutes non-stop", or whatever your goal is. This should habitually be your sure-fire way to build up self-esteem. You need an internal cheerleader when running, in order to meet the set milestone, and you need to train this cheerleader of yours to say motivating things to say to you, this (cheerleader) often is referred as positive self-talk. When you become habitual of self-talk, it not only gets you complete your running milestone, but would start soaking into the rest of your life and you would find yourself using it at work, while doing dishes and troublesome tasks would no longer appear hard to work on.

Like any goal in life, with running, you could set goals large and small. For the beginner runner, a good goal might be to complete in local 5k. You would without doubt enjoy the sense of accomplishment – not to mention the bragging rights at the office.

Always set realistic goals for running and you would build up your self-esteem – and miles – much faster.

Skills and Strengths

You all have acquired skills, talents all your life through education, sports, work and life in general and this background appears easier to analyse on the surface. But in reality, you need to do more in-depth evaluation of your skills.

Sit with self as discussed earlier and write up a detailed list of the skills and strengths your education/training have provided you. What is the skill set you have actually acquired? Ask yourself, if you are applying your skills and abilities to their full up extent?"

The most important thing is that you pursue your interests, convert some of them into hobbies, and turn at least one of them into a second profession. Enlist your core gifts like composure, compassion, conflict-resolution, self-control, perseverance or determination etc. and bring them to surface of professional life and these could become a major factor for you in achieving success.

You have to keep revisiting this skill set of yours regularly as this is not once in a lifetime exercise. As your keep progressing in life, regular review of your strengths would help you discover unknown strengths. Which would help you down the right path. And you have better possibility of striking gold.

De-cluttering for success

When you surrounded by unwanted things (called clutter) and disorder in your lives, it would make an excellent breeding ground for negativity, and this negativity is what brings about feelings of low self-worth and low self-esteem. This hinders you in life and could be the basis of you being unsuccessful in what you choose to do. Therefore, if we want to succeed and make the most out of life than you should de-clutter regularly and remove any excess obstacles and belongings from your path, keeping your lives open and free flowing. Here are few straightforward points to remember and practice to keep your home and life clutter free.

Replace old with new

Make this your mantra and apply it to everything you bring to your home clothing, utensils, furniture or any other item. If you continually keep buying and bringing new items, then very quickly you are going to run short of space to keep them all. You would be overrun with items, which end up being packed in cartons and put in the garage. You would say stuff in the garage is not taking any space. The items in the garage are still clutter, the clutter that you could do without. So, get into the habit of throwing things away or giving them to needy when you buy new.

Don't accumulate things

We all have the habit of accumulating things, which we have picked up unconsciously, it could be from our parents, grandparents or other elders. In this process we make our homes a storage place rather than a place to live and enjoy. We subconsciously believe that we need things but in reality, we do not, but still hang on to them. Your home is considered mirror reflection of your mental map and clearing unwanted things from your home would help in having a clearer thinking pattern.

You need to develop a habit of not keeping the unwanted things by developing the mental muscle that would help you. Build this muscle by getting rid of the small things first, you could start with throwing junk mail, flyers, old newspapers, magazines, letters or trash from your car. Develop the habit shredding the important unwanted letters straight away instead of keeping them, especially if you have an e-document for it. You should collect trash from your car on daily basis as well and bin it. You would be surprised by the results of this habit, when you find out how much junk you could eliminate from your home daily just by taking care of items like this.

And never hang onto unnecessary things simply because they are presents given to you by loved ones. But if you keep things just because they were given to you by someone but do not need them, you are just adding to the clutter. Sometimes you buy things, but you do not like them, return them or give it away to someone who likes them or sell it, but do not hang onto it.

Never procrastinate

We've all been there. You've been given 20 days to prepare for a presentation- yet you don't even start on the paper until the day before its due. This is called Procrastination. It is said that procrastination is the "dream killer", as it destroys productivity. Let's define procrastination:

Procrastination: putting off or postponing something to a later time.
Unconscious practice of procrastination would destroy your efficiency and eventually kill your dreams. Just reflect for a moment on what could you possibly accomplish (that's worth

accomplishing), if you do not fail to take action? Just like when you put off cleaning your house, you would eventually be living in a pig pin, and on top of this the health issues that could arise from poor maintenance.

Do not let procrastination murder your dream of being successful.

If you think there could be a miracle solution for this dream eater "procrastination", then you are in illusion. Only solution to this is to take action. Taking the required action when needed is the only solution for this. Most of you procrastinate when it is time to go for a run or work out but remember the time when you went out for run and you registered feeling better afterwards. Every Time you procrastinate, you feel guilty or even depressed at times. If you lack motivation to accomplish even the minimal tasks, you could be on borderline of depression or manically depressed. You always feel better when you get things done.

Procrastination can easily cause depression and you could experience bad health, relationships, poor grades, and average work performance. This all could lead to major loses in your life. You do not want these things happening to you, so why do they procrastinate?

Four Questions

Chapter 5
Four Questions !

As a Life/Transformational Coach, I ask my clients the following four questions. These questions have been effective tools for me as these help my clients to make sense of the things and feel good in the present moment. These questions could help you as well if you answer them with honesty. They are great to have in your arsenal for the times when you are upset and feel low in self-esteem. They're good in elevating your self-esteem and emotions to higher level in long run.

A. Ask yourself; What are the facts?

When a person walks into my office confused and really upset, this is the wonderful technique which I use and it has never failed to help; I ask them to describe their situation and environment prior to they got upset, slowly and in detail.

When your emotions are high, you tend to overlook the important factual details of your situation and environment because you're so consumed with how you feel. As a result, you fail to see some pretty obvious causes of your stress.

For example, I often listen to many of my clients describing a disturbing discussion they had with their partner in bed. Because they were so focused on the content of the argument and how they felt that they missed the fact that time was 11:00 PM! And they were late for bed just because of some baseless argument, which would have no meaning in the morning or maximum by end of the day. (this has always been surprising to me that how and from where these people get the strength to argue at that time of night.)

Me and my wife have made a pact that we never end our day with any sort of argument, no matter how small it may be. Because we have realized that we are living a life that has been loaned to us, and nobody knows when the recovery would happen. So, we go to bed on a good note and if anyone's loan deal expires, other won't have to live with the negative feelings that are associated with these sorts of experiences. We all have heard so many stories.

You better not ignore your situation just because your mind is screaming at you.

You had a long busy at work and feel really exhausted. And this is one of the major causes of you having an argument or a fight or getting upset with your partner, parents or children. Once you are able recognize this pattern of yours, it would slowly change, and you would become more empathetic and compassionate with yourselves and others when you're upset.

If you want to improve your understanding of your difficult emotions and mood, and improve your self-esteem along the way, start by slowing down and noticing "just the facts" of the situation.

You would be thinking how you can recognize the situation and "just notice the facts". There is a very simple formula; answer the four Ws. Absolutely, ask yourself When? Where? Who? What? And then slowly and consciously answer them.

You can ask.

When did you first felt upset?
Where were you when you noticed your mood changing?
Who you were interacting with before and during this shift?
What was going on, that made you feel upset?

"It is a capital mistake to theorize before one has data."

B. Check your emotional Temperature?

You can ask yourself; What is my emotional temperature?

You understand money, politics, football, technology much better than you understand your emotions. Some of you don't understand them at all. This is because your model of emotions, your beliefs about what emotions are and how they operate within you is out of sync with who you really are. Either this model is faulty, or it is outdated. Maybe it's not your model at all.

The most common mistake that all do, when it comes to your emotions is that you treat unhealthy emotions (pain, anger, sorrow) as they are some kind of disease, objects that need to be fixed or eliminated. Because you don't understand these emotions, it doesn't make them bad. There is nothing broken, so you don't need to fix anything. You just need to understand them, if you want to feel better, change your relationship with your emotions.

Let me share with you a simple trick that I learned in my very first Life Coaching course. This is a very simple trick that you could do and could relate to, which would help you have a different perspective about emotions. Compare your emotions to the lights on the dashboard of your car.

You all are aware of anxiety feeling when the low fuel light flashes on while you are on a motorway, some even get anxious when the petrol station is a mile away. Certainly, this impulsive eruption of anxiousness and fear is not good, but it should be considered useful to a certain extend.

Now think of what would you do the next time when your low-fuel light went off making you feel anxious and fearful, would you stick tape over it? You wouldn't, similarly you would not put sticky tape on your routine anxious problems, like the one we just discussed. Because you repeat them every time in the same situation, like getting anxious seeing the low fuel light.

When you put sticky tape on the fuel light, you would feel comfortable for a little while, but now you end up in the middle of nowhere with an empty tank, nowhere to go. This situation is far more serious than being anxious and driving to the petrol pump. Now you are stuck, situation is much worse now than in previous situation. You would be stranded on the side of the motorway for hours waiting for recovery or your dad to come pick you up.

Notice the problem with different perspective?

You need to understand that your emotions and dashboard light are not the problem, they are there to help. But when you keep avoiding these helpful signals from your feelings you tend to invite bigger trouble further down the road. Avoidance or temporary fixes are not the solution.

It is very simple because when you are constantly fighting with your emotions and feeling, they fight back with more strength. Majority of your persistent unhealthy and unhelpful emotions surface then you tend to indulge in fight with your feelings.

You are feeling sad, but you forcefully pretend not to feel sad. Once you have forced this on yourself, the internal film of self-talk begins; with the ways you should use, all the reasons you should feel happy about and stay content, all the errors you should have avoided, and so on.

When you feel anxious, your mind interpret that something bad is going to happen, and as a result next few hours are spent with worry and anxiety. Most of us love to take responsibility of other problems, we assume that we should have done something to help them, as a result we drag ourselves into a whirlwind of blame, self-anger, and sometimes depression.

From all these examples you could conclude that common denominator is your unhealthy and aggressive relationship with your own feelings. And you saw that when you regularly pick fights with your emotions, they are more likely to fight back.

- Problem-solving your anxiety leads to panic.
- Ruminating on your anger leads to rage.
- Criticizing your sadness leads to depression.

If you constantly struggle with painful emotions, difficult moods and low self-esteem, then there is a good chance that your relationship with your emotions is the problem, not the emotions themselves. Because treating an emotion as a problem teaches your brain to see it as a problem.

All of which means, you need to foster a better relationship with your emotions, especially the painful ones:

- Acknowledge your emotions instead of trying to fix them.
- Make friends your emotions rather than running away from them.
- Be curious about your emotions instead of interrogating them.

The next time you feel anxious, sad or guilty or any other painful feeling, try to see these emotions as lights on your board. This small change of thought prepares you for a much healthier, more productive and less painful relationship with your own emotions.

"Your emotions make you human. Even the unpleasant ones have a purpose. Don't lock them away. If you ignore them, they just get louder and angrier." — Sabaa Tahir

C. What's my story?

Now that you have learned to pause, to collect the facts about your situation, acknowledge your emotions with curiosity and kindness, you're ready to learn the third question: What's my story?

You are very good at creating stories, no matter what happens. You create stories when good happens, when bad happens and even when nothing happens. But when something not good or scary or unfavourable happens, the stories you create are about the event are nowhere near the actual fact.

In most cases the stories that are created in your head are negative and lead to negative self-talk, and it sounds somewhat like this in your head:

When you say something inappropriate, what goes in your mind is; "ugh… why I have to screw up every time. I'm a screw-up. I should have just kept your mouth shut!" But this is your belief that you have said something wrong, there is a possibility that the other person didn't even noticed, as most people are passive listeners, or they even liked what you said. You cook stories on your mind without any facts, unless you have some psychic mind reading powers.

Now the most common story of your life if you are married. After every little argument with you partner you say, "Why does he/she always have to be so sarcastic? It's like he/she doesn't even love me anymore. Getting into this relationship was a big mistake. We would never be happy…" But have you noticed that after some time you are in love with your partner again as if nothing has happened? You do this on repeat mode, but unconsciously.

Therefore, it is very important that you understand your habitual and sometimes automatic self-talk patterns, and this is the key to understanding why you feel the way you do and how to feel better. Your self-esteem is dependent on how you feel about yourself.

Your life is your story and you are the hero in this story of your life. Don't consider as a support artist or an extra like most people consider themselves. Not only that you are the hero of your story, you are the writer and the director. You are the musician of this life movie of yours. If you don't the story of your life you have the authority to redirect it the way you want it to be.

See, emotions are not discreet things that simply pop into our brains. They are experiences that you actively construct. You take incoming sensory information about what happened (the facts) then interpret those facts via thinking processes like self-talk (the story), and the result is an emotional experience that you've created.

It is true that, you can't always control what happened to us (events), and you can't always control what thoughts pop into mind (automatic thoughts), but you can control continued habits of thought like worry, rumination, self-judgment, and the like. And if you can learn to control this storytelling, you can exert a powerful level of control over how you end up feeling emotionally.

So, the next time when something upsetting happens and you feel the rush of strong emotions like fear or sadness, ask yourself:

- What's my story?

- What are the thoughts running through my mind?

- How well does my story fit the facts? Is my theory based on genuine evidence?

- Is there another story or theory that fits the facts better?

This approach to changing how you feel emotionally by changing the way you think about what happens is the backbone of cognitive behavioral therapy, one of the most effective approaches to treat and work through clinical struggles such as anxiety, depression, anger problems, etc. But it's not really new.

Long before cognitive behavioral therapy, mental health or psychiatric diagnoses were something, ancient philosophers and thinkers understood this basic concept: how we usually think determines how we usually feel.

The concept was perhaps best articulated by Epictetus; what really scares and dismays you are not the external events themselves, but the way you think about them. It is not things that bother you, but your interpretation of its meaning.

D: What do I really want?

So far, you have leaned three simple questions to discover the fundamental emotional formula of your lives.

Event + Story = Emotion

When you train to ask; what are the facts? What does my emotional thermometer tell you? And what is my story? You can begin to see the emotional machinery that influences your mood and how you feel.

The last and the most important of all the four question this is the one that I find the most important. when you ask this question to yourself, you need to be in calm state of mind. Really calm and relaxed within yourself. Go to a place where you feel relaxed, spend some time with yourself, have few deep breaths and ask yourself.

"What do I really want?"

You have to be really honest with yourself, it must be your answer. If it's not the answer from deep within you then you might end up feeling more pain and even much lower self-esteem. Nobody's vision for the good life is simply the absence of pain, because you all know, deep down, that happiness doesn't come from the mere absence of suffering.

My definition of good life is constant growth, learning and exploration. You need to figure out what is the purpose of your life and secondly what are the most things and people in your life. Once you have done this, you could easily go after them without any pain or suffering attached. You would be running like a sport car firing all cylinders and would never feel tired again. It would raise your self-esteem automatically. In simple words, it's all about your values.

You must know that emotions only determine the quality of your present moment, but your values determine the quality of your whole lives.

Over the years as a Mindfulness and Transformational coach, I have seen a particular behaviour, that most of my clients invest lot of effort and energy in becoming emotionally intelligent in order to handle their unhelpful habits and painful emotions. They invest loads of time and money in mastering this, but later they realize that this is temporary. There would be times when success comes, but for a bit. It's a lot easier to let go of worry when you have something else to focus about which you're genuinely excited and passionate about.

In the long run, emotional intelligence recognizes that life is much, much more than how we feel at any given time. All the complexity and nuances of our mental habits and emotional range are destined to live at the service of our values, our aspirations, the things we really want.

The solution for this temporary solution is that you ask yourself; What do I really want?

- What excites me and lights my fire?
- What are my dreams?
- What are my guiding values?
-

Ultimately, your happiness in daily life is much more than just relief of pain and suffering, it's about flourishing, living out your potential.

"There is but one cause of human failure, and that is man's lack of faith in his true Self." — *William James,* American philosopher

"Happiness is not a Goal……. It's a by-product of a Life Well-Lived."

- Eleanor Roosevelt

Printed in Poland
by Amazon Fulfillment
Poland Sp. z o.o., Wrocław